Second Edition

NEWS &

NUMBERS

Second Edition

NEWS &

NUMBERS

A guide to reporting statistical claims and controversies in health and other fields

Victor Cohn
FORMER SCIENCE EDITOR
Washington Post

Lewis Cope
FORMER SCIENCE REPORTER
Star Tribune of Minneapolis–St. Paul

FOREWORD BY Jay A. Winsten
Associate Dean for Public and Community Affairs and
the Frank Stanton Director of the Center for Health
Communication, Harvard School of Public Health

Iowa State Press
A Blackwell Publishing Company

Victor Cohn was a science writer at the *Washington Post* for 25 years, serving part of the time as science editor. The *New York Times* called Cohn "one of the country's top science writers." *Newsweek* had named him among seven "top newspaper science writers." He received numerous awards, including an honorary doctorate degree from Georgetown University. He started work on the first edition of this book as a visiting fellow at the Harvard School of Public Health. He worked actively on this new, revised edition until his death in 2000.

Lewis Cope, who spent 29 years as a science writer for the *Star Tribune* in Minneapolis–St. Paul, is coauthor of this new edition. Like Cohn, he received numerous national awards for his writing. Both Cohn and Cope are former presidents of the National Association of Science Writers.

© 2001 Victor Cohn and Lewis Cope; © 1989 Victor Cohn
All rights reserved.

Iowa State Press
A Blackwell Publishing Company
2121 State Avenue, Ames, Iowa 50014

Orders: 1-800-862-6657
Office: 1-515-292-0140
Fax: 1-515-292-3348
Web site: www.iowastatepress.com

⊚ Printed on acid-free paper in the United States of America

First edition, 1989
Second edition, 2001

Library of Congress Cataloging-in-Publication Data

Cohn, Victor, 1919–2000
    News & numbers: a guide to reporting statistical claims and controversies in health and other fields / Lewis Cope.—2nd ed.
        p. cm.
Includes bibliographical references and index.
    ISBN 0-8138-1424-3
    1. Public health—Statistics.   2. Environmental health—Statistics.
3. Vital statistics.   I. Title: News and numbers.   II. Title.
    RA407 .C64 2001
    362.1'021—dc21   2001002373

The last digit is the print number: 9 8 7 6 5 4 3 2

Contents

v

A Note to Our Readers

The rules of statistics are the rules of clear thinking, codified. They apply to any kind of reporting in which numbers—stated or implied—are involved: political reporting, science reporting, business, economics, sports, or whatever. This manual explains the logic and language of statistics, so we reporters (and other people as well) can ask better questions and get better answers.

Because this book began as a project of the Harvard School of Public Health, the reporting of health is emphasized. But the principles, and many of the "questions you can ask," can be used to assess claims and controversies in virtually any field. The final three chapters specifically show how.

—VICTOR COHN
—LEWIS COPE

A Tribute to Victor Cohn, 1919–2000

My father, Victor Cohn, had a wonderful and blessed life. He was a hard-working man who was passionate about his work. He loved being a reporter, believing that democracy requires an informed public—and because it was fun.

Shortly before his 70th birthday, the *Journal of the American Medical Association* interviewed him. He said in that interview that he would never really retire but would write about science and medicine for the rest of his life. He did.

At age 79, he was diagnosed with a fatal disease. He was in the middle of this edition of *News & Numbers,* and he was also planning to write yet one more book. The new book was to be called *The Wonders I've Seen* and would describe scientific and medical developments he had written about in a career lasting more than five decades, ending with his death at age 80, in the early weeks of the 21st century. And what wonders he saw! He was fortunate that the early days of his career coincided with the tremendous burst of scientific discoveries and accomplishments in post–World War II America. He wrote about them all, from the polio vaccine, to men on the moon, and on to human organs transplanted into the desperately ill.

But he was not only a path-breaking journalist who became the gold standard for science and medical reporting, he was also an unassuming man who came from simple working people and never forgot it. No wonder he earned his living looking for the truth, and writing about it in a way that ordinary people could understand. He also never forgot the people who helped him on his way up and, in turn, was always available to help young journalists. This book is a continuation of his determination to help reporters—including himself—do a better job.

He has left the extended Cohn family, three children and six grandchildren, with a priceless legacy of purpose in life and extraordinary integrity. Along with his many friends, we miss him.

Finally, I would be remiss if I did not note that nothing my father accomplished would have been possible without his teenage sweetheart, who became his wife. My beloved mother, Marcella Rigler Cohn, was the rock and foundation of a supportive and loving home, making it possible for him to go out into the world and accomplish so much.

—DEBORAH COHN RUNKLE

Victor was a master of his craft. As part of this, he showed journalists the importance of probing numbers to discover what they can tell us about virtually every aspect of our lives. He wrote *News & Numbers* to share his techniques for doing this in the most revealing and the most responsible way. With this new edition, Victor's messages will live on.

—LEWIS COPE, COAUTHOR OF THIS EDITION

Foreword

Now, more than ever, an informed public needs to comprehend scientific and medical research. This understanding is often difficult to achieve because mathematical statistics, a language of research, is outside the experience of the general public. For this reason, journalists are a vital link between the scientific world and the public. We all count on newspapers, magazines, television, and the Internet to tell us what the "latest findings" really mean. Accurate translation on the part of journalists is particularly important because scientists often lack the interest or skills necessary to explain their findings in language that can be readily understood by the general public.

News & Numbers is a guide for journalists who report on scientific and medical research, on risk, on polling—in short, on a variety of topics involving statistics. It is a necessary reference book for reporters to have on their desks when writing on deadline. This book will help them do a better job of educating the public.

News & Numbers, first published in 1989, and revised in 1994, has been reprinted nine times and translated into Japanese and Spanish. Victor Cohn's book grew out of the Media Project of the Health Science Policy Working Group of the Division of Health Policy Research and Education at Harvard University. He began work on the first edition while serving as a visiting fellow in the Center for Health Communication at the Harvard School of Public Health. When first approached about writing this book, Victor protested that he quit studying math after receiving a gentleman's D in high school geometry. In fact, he often said that the book's subtitle should be "Math Dummy Writes Book on Statistics." Victor's protests to the contrary, perhaps it took someone deservedly unassuming about his mathematical aptitude to write a book that his colleagues could understand.

In 1999, Victor, then a vigorous 79 years old, was hard at work on the second edition of *News & Numbers* when he was diagnosed with a fatal illness. He spent much of the nine months remaining to him ensuring that the book would be published. To that end, he sought the help of a long-time and much-admired colleague, Lewis Cope, formerly of the *Star Tribune* of Minneapolis–St. Paul. The result is a modernized, easily readable second edition that builds on and extends the usefulness of the first edition.

Victor Cohn was my friend and colleague, and I, along with his many friends, miss him terribly. But he has left us three meaningful legacies. One is the Victor Cohn Prize for Excellence in Medical Science Reporting, established by the Council for the Advancement of Science Writing, an educational organization cofounded by Victor in 1959. The second legacy is this new edition of *News & Numbers*. The third is the profound impact he had on the emergence and maturation of the field of science reporting. Victor served as a mentor to an entire generation of science writers. His impact will be reflected in their work for a long time to come.

—JAY A. WINSTEN, Associate Dean for Public and
Community Affairs and the Frank Stanton
Director of the Center for Health Communication,
Harvard School of Public Health

Condensed from the Foreword to the 1989 Edition

Reporters play an essential role in communicating science to the public. In common with scientists, they desire accuracy. The biostatistics that scientists must use present special problems. This gives uncommon and misleading meanings to common words like "significant" and "power." Mathematical statistics often produce results that are disturbingly counterintuitive, at least at first, to laymen and scientists alike.

Victor Cohn of the *Washington Post* has prepared this manual to help reporters cut through such statistical tangles. Faculty members of the Harvard School of Public Health have been able to help him produce this book as a visiting fellow and as a contributor to the Health Science Policy Working Group.

By such efforts, scientists and writers may gradually upgrade the whole communication system, scientific and journalistic. Thus we may clear the communication channel between science and the public.

—FREDERICK MOSTELLER, the Robert I. Lee
Professor Emeritus of Mathematical Statistics,
Harvard University

Acknowledgments

Victor Cohn's main mentor and guide in preparation of the first edition of this book was Dr. Frederick Mosteller of the Harvard School of Public Health. The project was supported by the Russell Sage Foundation and by the Council for the Advancement of Science Writing.

Cohn did much of the original work as a visiting fellow at the Harvard School of Public Health, where Dr. Jay Winsten, director of the Center for Health Communications, was another indispensable guide and Drs. John Bailar III, Thomas A. Louis, and Marvin Zelen were valuable helpers, as were Drs. Gary D. Friedman and Thomas M. Vogt at the Kaiser organizations; Michael Greenberg at Rutgers University; and Peter Montague of Princeton University. (For those who aided Cohn with the first edition of this book, listed in this paragraph and elsewhere in these acknowledgments, the universities and other affiliations cited are at the time of that edition's publication.)

Others helped Cohn and his coauthor, Lewis Cope, in expanding sections of the book for this new edition. The authors appreciate the great help of Dr. Michael Osterholm, Infection Control Advisory Network, Inc. (ican, inc.), for his wise council on epidemiology. They thank Rob Daves, director of the Minnesota Poll at the *Star Tribune* in Minneapolis–St. Paul, for his help in adding a chapter on polling.

Special thanks go to Cohn's daughter Deborah Cohn Runkle, a senior program associate at the American Association for the Advancement of Science and a fine statistician, and to Cope's daughter Mary Amelia Fitzharris, a fine editor.

Others who provided valuable counsel for this new edition include John Ullmann, executive director of the World Press Institute at Macalester College in St. Paul; Dr. Phyllis Wingo of the American Cancer Society; and Drs. Margaret Wang and Ching Wang at the University of Missouri–Columbia.

Many other people helped with the first edition of the book. Thanks go to Drs. Stuart A. Bessler, Syntex Corporation; H. Jack Geiger, City University of New York; Nicole Schupf Geiger, Manhattanville College; Arnold Relman, *New England Journal of Medicine;* Eugene Robin, Stanford University; and Sidney Wolfe, Public Citizen Health Research Group. Thanks also go to Katherine Wallman, Council of Professional Association on Federal Statistics; Howard L. Lewis, American Heart Association; Philip Meyer, University of North Carolina; Lynn Ries, National Cancer Institute; Mildred Spencer Sanes; and Earl Ubell. Also Harvard's Drs. Peter Braun, Harvey Fineberg, Howard Frazier, Howard Hiatt, William Hsaio, Herb Sherman, and William Stason.

Cohn thanks his editors and colleagues at the *Washington Post,* and Cope thanks their counterparts at the *Star Tribune* in Minneapolis—particularly the *Star Tribune*'s great library staff.

This new work was aided by the Robert Wood Johnson Foundation, the Esther A. and Joseph Klingenstein Fund, and the American Statistical Association, with additional help from the Commonwealth Fund and Georgetown University.

Despite all this great help, any misstatements remain the authors' responsibility.

Second Edition

NEWS &

NUMBERS

Where We Can Do Better

1

Facts and Figures! Put 'em Down!

—Charles Dickens (in *The Chimes*)

There are lies, there are damned lies, and there are statistics.

—Attributed to Disraeli

Almost everyone has heard that "figures don't lie, but liars can figure." We need statistics, but liars give them a bad name, so to be able to tell the liars from the statisticians is crucial.

—Dr. Robert Hooke

A doctor reports that he has developed a promising, even exciting new treatment. Is the claim justified, or could there be some other explanation for his patients' improvement? Are there too few patients to justify *any* claim?

An environmentalist says that a certain toxic waste will cause many cases of cancer. An industry spokesman denies it. What research has been done? What are the numbers? How valid are they?

Nutritional advice, technology, crime rates, other risk warnings, and weather forecasts all rely on numbers. Even when we journalists say we are dealing in facts and ideas, much of what we report is based on numbers. Politics comes down to votes. Budgets and dollars dominate government. Business, employment, sports, polls, and educational assessments all demand numbers.

While *News & Numbers* is written primarily to aid news reporters in ferreting meaning out of numbers, this manual should be useful for other people as well. We can all be better citizens if we act sensibly on the numbers that we read and hear. This book can help anyone answer three questions about all sorts of studies and statistical claims: What can I believe? What does it mean? How can I explain it to others?

We can be better reporters and better citizens if we understand how the best statisticians—the best figurers— think. This manual focuses on how they probe possible biases and other factors that sometimes mislead, to separate the wheat from the chaff of numbers. You can do the same. And a welcome surprise: You can do it without any heavy-lifting math!

The Challenge

The very way that we reporters tell our readers or viewers about a medical, environmental, or other controversy can affect the outcome.

If we ignore a bad situation, the public may suffer. If we write "danger," the public may quake. If we write "no danger," the public may be falsely reassured.

If we paint an experimental medical treatment too brightly, the public is given false hope. If we are overly critical of some new drug, people may avoid a treatment that could help them, maybe even save their lives.

But numbers offered by experts sometimes conflict, thus confusing us and triggering controversies. Statistics are used or misused even by people who tell us, "I don't believe in statistics," then claim that all of us or most people or many do such and such. We should not merely repeat such numbers, stated or implied, but also interpret them to deliver the best possible picture of reality.

And whether we reporters will it or not, we have in effect become part of the regulatory apparatus. Dr. Peter Montague at Princeton University tells us: "The environmental and toxic situation is so complex, we can't possibly have enough officials to monitor it. Reporters help officials decide where to focus their activity."

"Journalists opened up" the Love Canal toxic waste issue by "independent investigation," said Dr. Dorothy Nelkin at Cornell University. "The extensive press coverage contributed to investigations that eventually forced the re-staffing of the Environmental Protection Agency and the creation of a national toxic waste disposal program."[1] That very coverage, however, may also have stampeded public officials into hasty studies that left unanswered the crucial question: Did the Love Canal wastes actually cause birth defects and other physical problems?[2]

Four Areas for Improvement

As we reporters seek to make page one or the six o'clock news:

1. We sometimes overstate and oversimplify. We may report, "A study showed that black is white," when a study merely suggested that there was some evidence that such might be the case. We may slight or omit the fact that a scientist calls a result "preliminary." As scientific unsophisticates, we may confuse a study that merely suggests a hypothesis that should be investigated—very often the case—with a study that presents strong and convincing evidence.

Philip Meyer, veteran reporter and author of *Precision Journalism,* writes, "Journalists who misinterpret statistical data usually tend to err in the direction of over-interpretation. . . . The reason for this professional bias is self-evident; you usually can't write a snappy lead upholding [the negative]. A story purporting to show that apple pie makes you sterile is more interesting than one that says there is no evidence that apple pie changes your life."[3]

We've said, tongue only partly in cheek, that there are only two types of health news stories—New Hope and No Hope. In truth, we must remember that the truth usually lies somewhere in the middle.

2. We work fast, sometimes too fast, with severe limits on the space or airtime we may fill. We find it hard to tell editors or news directors, "I haven't had enough time. I don't have the story yet." Even a long-term project or special may be hurriedly done. In a newsroom, "long term" may mean a few weeks. A major Southern newspaper had to print a front-page retraction after a series of stories alleged that people who worked at or lived near a plutonium plant suffered in excess numbers from a blood disease. "Our reporters obviously had confused statistics and scientific data," the editor admitted. "We did not ask enough questions."[4]

3. We too often omit essential perspective, context, or background. Dr. Thomas Vogt at the Kaiser Permanente Center for Health Research tells of seeing the headline "Heart Attacks from Lack of 'C'" and then, two months later, "People Who Take Vitamin C Increase Their Chances of a Heart Attack."[5] Both stories were based on limited, far-from-conclusive animal studies.

It's not only what we write, it's what we emphasize. A National Institutes of Health (NIH) National

Cancer Institute (NCI) survey indicated that many people refuse to consider healthy changes in lifestyle because they think "carcinogens are everywhere in the environment." People may have read or heard that most cancers are "environmentally related." Reporters should emphasize that this is a very broad category. In the opinion of most informed scientists, most "environmental" cancers are related mainly to individual behavior, outstandingly smoking and probably nutritional factors.[6] Many scientific studies indicate that simply eating more fruits, vegetables, and grains can help protect against various types of cancer.[7]

We tend to rely most on "authorities" who are either most quotable or quickly available or both. They often tend to be those who get most carried away with their sketchy and unconfirmed but "exciting" data—or have big axes to grind, however lofty their motives. The cautious, unbiased scientist who says, "Our results are inconclusive" or "We don't have enough data yet to make any strong statement" or "I don't know" tends to be omitted or buried deep down in the story. And yes, some scientists do overstate—but bad science is no excuse for bad journalism.

4. We are influenced by intense competition and other pressures to tell the story first and tell it most dramatically. One reporter said, "The fact is, you are going for the strong [lead and story]. And, while not patently absurd, it may not be the lead you would go for a year later."[8]

Or even a few hours later. Witness the rush to declare a winner on election night in the Bush-Gore presidential race (more about this in Chapter 10, on polling and related numbers).

We are also subject to human hope and human fear. A new "cure" comes along, and we want to believe it. A new alarm is sounded, and we too tremble. Alarms also make good news. We too often obey a sardonic maxim: Bad news is good news; good news is no news. Dr. H. Jack Geiger, a respected former science writer who became a professor of medicine, says:

I know I wrote stories in which I explained or interpreted the results wrongly. I wrote stories that didn't have the disclaimers I should have written. I wrote stories under competitive pressure, when it became clear later that I shouldn't have written them. I wrote stories when I hadn't asked—because I didn't know enough to ask—"Was your study capable of getting the answers you wanted? Could it be interpreted to say something else? Did you take into account possible confounding factors?"

How can we learn to do better?

The Certainty of Uncertainty

2

> Too much of the science reporting in the press [blurs] what we're sure of and what we're not very sure of and what is inconclusive. The notion of tentativeness tends to drop out of much reporting.
>
> —Dr. Harvey Brooks

> The only trouble with a sure thing is the uncertainty.
>
> —Author unknown

Scientists keep changing their minds.

They tell us air bags in cars can save lives, then that air bags sometimes kill small children when the bags pop out in crashes.

They tell us that coffee does or doesn't cause various medical problems, time after time offering different advice. They tell us that a drug works fine, then take it off the market because it's too risky to use.

They tell us to worry about cholesterol in our bloodstream, then that there is some good cholesterol along with bad cholesterol. And after we've learned to read food labels, the U.S. Food and Drug Administration (FDA) announced plans in late 1999 to change them, adding trans fatty acids* as a newly recognized heart risk.[1]

They come up with one theory after another about the extinction of the dinosaurs.

To some people, this switching gives science a bad name. Actually, it's science working just as it's supposed to work.

The first thing that you should understand about science is that it is almost always uncertain. The scientific process allows science to move ahead without waiting for an elusive "proof positive." Patients can be offered a new treatment at the point that there's a good probability that it works.

How can science afford to act on less than certainty? Because science is a continuing story—always retesting ideas. One scientific finding leads scientists to conduct more research, which may support and expand on the original finding. In medicine, this often allows more and more patients to benefit.

But in other cases, the continuing research results in modified conclusions. Or less often, in entirely new conclusions.

Remember "strict bed rest" to treat various ills? And the "ulcer diets"? And when a radical mastectomy was considered the only good way to treat breast cancer? These and many other treatments once seemed right, then were dropped after statistically rigorous comparisons with new ideas. We can guarantee one thing: Some treatments in use today will fall by the wayside as we move through the 21st century.

The Scientific Method

Let's step back and take a step-by-step look at the scientific way:

A scientist, seeking to explain or understand something—be it the behavior of an atom or the effect of the toxic chemicals at a Love Canal—usually proposes a hypothesis, then seeks to test it by experiment or observation. If the evidence is strongly supportive, the hypothesis may then become a theory or at some point even a law, like the law of gravity.

A theory may be so solid that it is generally accepted. *Example:* The theory that cigarette smoking causes lung cancer, for which almost any reasonable person would say the case has been proved, for all practical purposes.

The phrase "for all practical purposes" is important, for scientists, being practical people, must often speak at two levels: the strictly scientific level and the level of ordinary reason that we require for daily guidance.

Example of the two levels: In June 1985, 16 forensic experts examined the bones that were supposedly those of the "Angel of Death," Dr. Josef Mengele. Dr. Lowell Levine, representing the U.S. Department of Justice, then said, "The skeleton is that of Josef Mengele within a reasonable scientific certainty," and Dr. Marcos Segre of the University of Sao Paulo, explained, "We deal with the law of probabilities. We are scientists and not magicians." Pushed by reporters' questions, several of the pathologists said they had "absolutely no doubt" of their findings.[2] (Later evidence made the case even stronger.)

Yet the most that any scientist can scientifically say— say with certainty in almost any such case—is: There is a very strong probability that such and such is true.

"When it comes to almost anything we say," reports Dr. Arnold Relman, former editor of the *New England Journal of Medicine,* "you, the reporter, must realize—and must help the public understand—that we are almost always dealing with an element of uncertainty. Most scientific information is of a probable nature, and we are only talking about probabilities, not certainty. What we are concluding is the best we can do, our best opinion at the moment, and things may be updated in the future."

Example: Until 1980 the American Cancer Society recommended that women have an annual Pap smear to detect cervical cancer. The recommendation was then changed to every three years for many women, after two initial examinations. Statistical studies had shown that this would be equally effective. The American Cancer Society's position now: "After three or more consecutive annual exams with normal findings, the Pap test may be performed less frequently at the discretion of the physician."[3]

And that, too, might be modified in the future. Two new studies published in 2000 in the *Journal of the American Medical Association* conclude that a new, easier-to-use test is more accurate than the Pap test for women over age 40. This new test, which doesn't require a pelvic exam, looks for the papilloma virus, which plays a key role in this type of cancer. Only time—and more research—can determine this new test's future role for women.[4]

Nature is complex, and almost all methods of observation and experiment are imperfect. "There are flaws in all studies," says Harvard's Dr. Marvin Zelen.[5] There may be weaknesses, often unavoidable ones, in the way a study is designed or conducted. Observers are subject to human bias and error. Measurements fluctuate.

"Fundamentally," writes Dr. Thomas Vogt, "all scientific investigations require confirmation, and until it is forthcoming all results, no matter how sound they may seem, are preliminary."[6]

But when study after study reach the same conclusion, confidence can grow. Scientists call this *replication* of the findings. We call it the way that science grows by building on itself.

Still, some uncertainty almost always prevails. Even when the test of time provides overwhelming evidence that a treatment really does help, there may be questions about how much it helps. Or just which patients should get the treatment. Or about side effects, or about something else. And if an "improved" treatment comes along, whether it's really better than the original treatment.

The bottom line for journalists covering all types of research: Good reporters try to tell their readers and viewers the degree of uncertainty, whether it's about a medical research finding or the effects of global warming. And wise reporters often use words like "may" and "evidence indicates," and seldom use words like "proof." A newspaper or TV report that contains needed cautions and caveats is a more credible report than one that doesn't.

Focusing on Medicine

Medicine, in particular, is full of disagreement and controversy. The reasons are many:

There's the lack of funds to mount enough trials. There's sometimes a lack of enough patients at any one center to mount a meaningful trial, particularly for rare diseases. There is the expense of doing multicenter trials. There's the swift evolution and obsolescence of some medical techniques.

There's the fact that, with the best of intentions, medical data—histories, physical examinations, interpretations of tests, descriptions of symptoms and diseases—are too often inexact and vary from physician to physician. And there are serious ethical obstacles to trying a new procedure when an old one is doing some good, or to experimenting on children, pregnant women, or the mentally ill.

Studies have found that many articles in prestigious medical journals have shaky statistics, and a lack of any explanation of such important matters as patients' complications and the number of patients lost to follow-up. Research papers presented at medical meetings, many of them widely reported by the media, raise more questions. Some are mere progress reports on incomplete studies. Some state tentative results that later collapse. Some are given to draw comment or criticism, or to get others interested in a provocative but still uncertain finding.[7]

The upshot, according to Dr. Gary Friedman at the Kaiser organization's Permanente Medical Group: "Much of health care is based on tenuous evidence and incomplete knowledge."[8]

In general, possible risks tend to be underestimated and possible benefits overestimated. Occasionally, unscrupulous investigators falsify their results. More often, they may wittingly or unwittingly play down data that contradict their theories, or they may search out statistical methods that give them the results they want. Before ascribing fraud, says Harvard's Dr. Frederick Mosteller, "keep in mind the old saying that most institutions have enough incompetence to explain almost any results."[9]

But don't despair. In medicine and other fields alike, the inherent uncertainties of science need not stand in the way of good sense. To live—to survive on this globe, to maintain our health, to set public policy, to govern ourselves—we almost always must act on the basis of incomplete or uncertain information. There is a way we can do so, as the next two chapters explain.

Testing the Evidence

3

Somehow the wondrous promise of the Earth is that there are things beautiful in it, things wondrous and alluring, and by virtue of your trade, you want to understand them.

—Mitchell Feigenbaum, Cornell University physicist and mathematician

The great tragedy of Science (is) the slaying of a beautiful hypothesis by an ugly fact.

—Thomas Henry Huxley

You can drown in the middle of a lake with an *average* depth of four feet.

—Author unknown

A father noticed that every time any of his 11 kids dropped a piece of bread on the floor, it landed with the buttered side up. "This utterly defies the laws of chance," the father exclaimed.

He just needed to ask one good question: Is there some other explanation for this buttered-side-up phenomenon? Close examination disclosed that his kids were buttering both sides of their bread.

Experts call this the failure to consider an alternate explanation. We call it the need for clear thinking.

Other examples that illustrate the need to think clearly before reaching conclusions:

• You may say that there's only a one-in-a-million chance that something will happen today. But remember, "an event with a one-in-a-million chance of happening to any American on any given day will, in fact, occur 260 times each day in this country" of more than 260 million Americans, says John Allen Paulos, a mathematics professor at Temple University.[1]

Experts call this the *Law of Small Probabilities*. We call it the Law of Unusual Events.

• Someone might look at professional basketball players and conclude that this sport makes people grow tall. Or look at the damage wreaked on mobile home parks by tornadoes, then conclude that mobile home parks cause tornadoes.[2]

Experts call this falsely concluding that association proves causation. We just call it crazy thinking.

Laugh if you must. These three examples illustrate some of the basic principles of good statistical analysis.

How to Search for the Truth

How can we reporters tell the facts, or the probable facts, from misleading and mistaken claims? We can borrow from science. We can try to judge all possible claims of fact by the same methods and rules of evidence that scientists use to derive some reasonable guidance in scores of unsettled issues. As a start, we can ask:

How do you know?

Have the claims been subjected to any studies or experiments? Or are you just citing some limited evidence, to suggest that a real study be conducted?

If studies have been done, were they acceptable ones, by general agreement? Were they without any substantial bias?

Are your results fairly consistent with those from related studies, and with general knowledge in the field?

Have the findings resulted in a consensus among other experts in the same field? Do at least the majority of informed persons agree? Or should we withhold (or strongly condition) our judgment until there is more evidence?

Are the conclusions backed by believable statistical evidence? And what is the degree of certainty or uncertainty? How sure can you be?

Most importantly, much of statistics involves clear thinking rather than numbers. And much, at least much of the statistical principles that reporters can most readily apply, is good sense.

There are many definitions of statistics as a tool. A few useful ones: The science and art of gathering, analyzing, and interpreting data. A means of deciding whether an effect is real, rather than the result of chance. A way of extracting information from a mass of raw data.

Statistics can be manipulated by charlatans and self-deluders. And good people make some mistakes along with their successes. Deciding on the truth of a matter can be difficult for the best statisticians, and sometimes no decision is possible. Some degree of uncertainty will ever rule in some situations, and lurk in almost all.

In some fields, for some things, no numbers are needed. "Edison had it easy," says Dr. Robert Hooke, a statistician and author. "It doesn't take statistics to see that a light has come on."[3] While examples in medicine are rare, it didn't take statistics to tell physicians that the first antibiotics cured infections that until then had been highly fatal.

Overwhelmingly, however, the use of statistics, based on probability, is called the soundest method of decision making. And the use of large numbers of cases, statistically analyzed, is called the only means for determining the unknown cause of many events.

Example: Birth control pills were tested on several hundred women, yet the pills had to be used for several years by millions before it became unequivocally clear that some women would develop heart attacks or strokes. The pills had to be used for some years more before it became clear that the greatest risk was to women who smoked and women over 35.

The best statisticians, along with practitioners on the firing line (e.g., physicians), often have trouble deciding when a study is adequate or meaningful. Most of us cannot become statisticians, but we can at least learn that there are studies and studies, and the unadorned claim that "we made a study" or "we did an experiment" may not mean much. We can learn to ask better questions if we understand some basic facts about scientific studies. These are four bedrock statistical concepts:

1. **Probability** (including the Law of Unusual Events)
2. **"Power" and numbers**
3. **Bias and "other explanations"**
4. **Variability**

We'll take them one by one.

How Probable Is It?

Scientists cope with uncertainty by measuring probabilities. All experimental results and all events can be influenced by chance, and almost nothing is 100 percent certain in science and medicine and life. So probabilities sensibly describe what has happened and should happen in the future under similar conditions. Aristotle said the probable "is what usually happens," but he might have added that the improbable happens more often than most of us realize.

The accepted numerical expression of probability in evaluating scientific and medical studies is the *P* (or *probability*) value. The *P* value is one of the most important figures a reporter should look for. It is determined by a statistical formula that takes into account the numbers of people or events being compared (the more the better) to answer the question: Could a difference or result this great or greater have occurred just by chance alone?

A low *P* value means a low probability that chance alone was at work. It means, for example, that there is a low probability that a medical treatment might have been declared beneficial when in truth it was not.

In a nutshell, the lower the *P* value, the more likely that a study's findings are "true" results and not due to chance alone.

The *P* value is expressed either as an exact number or as < .05, say, or > .05. This means "less than" or "greater than" a 5 percent probability that the observed result could have happened just by chance—or, to use a more elegant statistician's phrase, by *random variation*.

Here is how the *P* value is used to evaluate results:

- By convention, a *P* value of .05 or less, meaning there are only 5 or fewer chances in 100 that the result could have happened by chance, is most often regarded as low. This value is usually called *statistically significant* (though sometimes other values are used). The unadorned term "statistically significant" usually implies that *P* is .05 or less.

• A higher *P* value, one greater than .05, is usually seen as not statistically significant. The higher the value, the more likely the result is due to chance.

In common language and ordinary logic, a low chance of chance alone calling the shots means "it's close to certain." A strong chance that chance could have ruled means "it almost certainly can't be."

Why the number .05 or less? Partly for standardization. People have agreed that this is a good cutoff point for most purposes.

And partly out of common sense. Harvard's Mosteller tells us that if you toss a coin repeatedly in a college class and after each toss ask the class if there is anything suspicious going on, "hands suddenly go up all over the room" after the fifth head or tail in a row. There happens to be only one chance in 16—.0625, not far from .05, or 5 chances in 100—that five heads or tails in a row will show up in five tosses. "So there is some empirical evidence that the rarity of events in the neighborhood of .05 begins to set people's teeth on edge."[4]

Another common way of reporting probability is to calculate a *confidence level,* as well as a *confidence interval* (or *confidence limits* or *range*). This is what happens when a political pollster reports that candidate X would now get 50 percent of the vote and thereby lead candidate Y by 3 percentage points, "with a 3-percentage-point margin of error plus or minus at the 95 percent confidence level." In other words, Mr. or Ms. Pollster is 95 percent confident that X's share of the vote would be someplace between 53 and 47 percent. In a close election, that margin of error could obviously turn a candidate who is trailing in the poll into the election day victor.

The larger the number of subjects (patients or other participants) in a study, the greater the chance of a high confidence level and a narrow, and therefore more reassuring, confidence interval.

No matter how reassuring they sound, *P* values and confidence statements cannot be taken as gospel, for .05 is not a guarantee, just a number. There are important reasons for this:

> • **False positives**—All that *P* values measure is the *probability* that the experimental results could be the product of chance alone. In 20 experiments that report a positive finding at a *P* value of .05, one of these findings will be the result of chance alone. This is called a false positive. For example, a treatment may appear to be helping patients when it really isn't.

Dr. Marvin Zelen pointed to the many clinical (patient) trials of cancer treatment underway today. If the conventional value of .05 is adopted as the upper permissible limit for false positives, then every 100 studies with no actual benefit may, on average, produce 5 false-positive results, leading physicians down false paths.[5]

Many false positives are discovered by follow-up studies, but others may remain unrecognized. Relatively few studies are done that exactly repeat original studies; scientists aren't keen on spending their time to confirm someone else's work, and medical journals aren't keen on publishing them. But treatments are usually retested to try modifications and to expand uses, or sometimes to try to settle controversies.

> • **False negatives**—An unimpressive *P* value may simply mean that there were too few subjects to detect a real effect. This results in false negatives—missing an effective treatment (or some other effect or result) when it really exists.

In statistical parlance, by the way, a false positive is a Type I error (finding a result when it's not there), and a false negative is a Type II error (not finding a result when it is there).

- **Questions about cause and effect**—Statistical significance alone does not mean that there is cause and effect. *Association* or *correlation* is only a clue of possible cause.

Remember the rooster who thought he made the sun rise?

Just because a virus is found in patients with disease X doesn't mean it's the cause; the disease may have weakened their immune systems in a way that allowed the virus to gain a foothold. Just because people who work with a chemical develop a disease doesn't mean the chemical is the cause; the culprit may be something else in their workplace, or something not in the workplace at all.

In all such cases, more evidence is needed to confirm cause and effect (more about this in Chapter 5). To statisticians, by the way, association simply means there is at least a possible relationship between two things. A correlation is a measure of the association.

- **"Significant" versus important**—Highly "significant" *P* values can sometimes adorn unimportant differences in large samples. An impressive *P* value might also be explained by some other variable or variables—other conditions or associations—not taken into account.

Also, statistical significance does not necessarily mean biological, clinical, or practical significance. Inexperienced reporters sometimes see or hear the word "significant" and jump to that conclusion, even reporting that the scientists called their study "significant."

Example: A tiny difference between two large groups in mean hemoglobin concentration, or red blood count, may be statistically significant yet medically meaningless.[6]

And eager scientists can consciously or unconsciously "manipulate" the *P* value by choosing to compare different end points in a study (say, the patients' condition on leaving the hospital rather than length of survival) or by choosing the way the *P* value is calculated or reported.

There are several mathematical paths to a *P* value, such as the *chi-square,* the paired *t* test, and others. All can be legitimate. But be warned. Dr. David Salsburg at Pfizer, Inc., has written in the *American Statistician* of the unscrupulous practitioner who "engages in a ritual known as 'hunting for *P* values.' " Such a person finds ways to modify the original data to "produce a rich collection of small *P* values" even if those that result from simply comparing two treatments "never reach the magical .05."[7]

A researcher at a major medical center contributes: "If you look hard enough through your data, if you do enough subset analyses, if you go through 20 subsets, you can find one"—say, "the effect of chemotherapy on premenopausal women with two to five lymph nodes"—"with a *P* value less than .05. And people do this."

"Statistical tests provide a basis for probability statements," writes the University of Chicago's Dr. John Bailar, "only when the hypothesis is fully developed before the data are examined. . . . If even the briefest glance at a study's results moves the investigator to consider a hypothesis not formulated before the study was started, that glance destroys the probability value of the evidence at hand." (At the same time, Bailar adds, "review of data for unexpected clues . . . can be an immensely fruitful source of ideas" for new hypotheses "that can be tested in the correct way." And occasionally "findings may be so striking that independent confirmation . . . is superfluous.")[8]

Expect Some Unexpected Events

The laws of probability also teach us to expect some unusual, even impossible-sounding events.

We've all taken a trip to New York or London or someplace and bumped into someone from home. The chance of that? We don't know, but if you and a friend tossed for a drink every day after work, the chance that your friend would ever win 10 times in a row is 1 in 1,024. Yet your friend would probably do so sometime in a four- or five-year period.

While we call it the Law of Unusual Events, statisticians call it the *Law of Small Probabilities*. By whatever name, it tells us that a few people with apparently fatal illnesses will inexplicably recover. It tells us that there will be some amazing clusters of cases of cancer or birth defects that will have no common cause. And it tells us that we may once in a great while bump into a friend far from home.

In a large enough population such coincidences are not unusual. They produce striking anecdotes and often striking news stories. In the medical world they produce unreliable, though often cited, testimonial or anecdotal evidence. "The world is large," Thomas M. Vogt notes, "and one can find a large number of people to whom the most bizarre events have occurred. They all have personal explanations. The vast majority are wrong."[9]

"We [reporters] are overly susceptible to anecdotal evidence," Philip Meyer writes. "Anecdotes make good reading, and we are right to use them. . . . But we often forget to remind our readers—and ourselves—of the folly of generalizing from a few interesting cases. . . . The statistic is hard to remember. The success stories are not."[10]

Appreciate the "Power" of Big Numbers

This gets us to a related statistical concept of *power*. Statistically, power means the probability of finding something if it's there. For example, given that there is a true effect, say a difference between two medical treatments or an increase in cancer caused by a toxin in a group of workers, how likely are we to find it?

Sample size confers power. Statisticians say, "There is no probability until the sample size is there" . . . "Large numbers confer power" . . . "Large numbers at least make us sit up and take notice."*

All this concern about sample size can also be expressed as the *Law of Large Numbers,* which says that as the number of cases increases, the probable truth of a conclusion or forecast increases. The *validity* (truth or accuracy) and *reliability* (reproducibility) of the statistics begin to converge on the truth.

We already learned this when we talked about probability. But statisticians think of power as a function of both sample size and the accuracy of measurement, since that too affects the probability of finding something. Doing that, we can see that if the number of treated patients is small in a medical study, a shift from success to failure in only a few patients could dramatically decrease the success rate.

Example: If six patients have been treated with a 50 percent success rate, the shift to the failure column of just one patient would cut the success rate to 33 percent. And the total number is so small in any case that the result has little reliability. The result might be valid or accurate, but it would not be generalizable—it would not have reliability until confirmed by careful studies in larger samples.

The larger the sample, assuming there have been no fatal biases or other flaws, the more confidence a statistician would have in the result.

One science reporter said he has a quick, albeit far from definitive, screening test that he calls "my rule of two": He often looks at the key numbers, then adds or subtracts two from them. For example, someone says there are five cases of some form of cancer among workers in a company. Would it seem meaningful if there were three?

A statistician says, "This can help with small numbers but not large ones." Mosteller contributes "a little trick I use a lot on counts of any size." He explains, "Let's say some political unit has 10,000 crimes or deaths or accidents this year. Has something new happened? The *minimum standard deviation* for a number like that is 100—that is, the square root of the original number. That means the number may vary by a minimum of 200 every year without even considering growth, the business cycle, or any other effect. This will supplement your reporter's approach." More about this later in this chapter.

False negatives—missing an effect where there is one—are particularly common when there are small numbers.

"There are some very well conducted studies with small numbers, even five patients, in which the results are so clear-cut that you don't have to worry about power," says Dr. Relman. "You still have to worry about applicability to a larger population, but you don't have to doubt that there was an effect. When results are negative, however, you have to ask, How large would the effect have to be to be discovered?"

Many scientific and medical studies are underpowered—that is, they include too few cases. "Whenever you see a negative result," another scientist says, "you should ask, What is the power? What was the chance of finding the result if there was one?" One study found that an astonishing 70 percent of 71 well-regarded clinical trials that reported no effect had too few patients to show a 25 percent difference in outcome. Half of the trials could not have detected a 50 percent difference.[11]

A statistician scanned an article on colon cancer in a leading journal. "If you read the article carefully," he said, "you will see that if one treatment was better than the other—if it would increase median survival by 50 percent, from five to seven and a half years, say—they had only a 60 percent chance of finding it out. That's little better than tossing a coin!"

The weak power of that study would be expressed numerically as .6, or 60 percent. Scan an article's fine print or footnotes, and you will sometimes find such a *power statement.*

How large is a large enough sample? One statistician calculated that a trial has to have 50 patients before there is even a 30 percent chance of finding a 50 percent difference in results.

Sometimes large populations indeed are needed.[12]

Examples: If some kind of cancer usually strikes 3 people per 2,000, and you suspect that the rate is quadrupled in people exposed to substance X, you would have to study 4,000 people for the observed excess rate to have a 95 percent chance of reaching statistical significance. The likelihood that a 30-to-39-year-old woman will suffer a myocardial infarction, or heart attack, while taking an oral contraceptive is about 1 in 18,000 per year. To be 95 percent sure of observing at least one such event in a one-year trial, you would have to observe nearly 54,000 women.[13]

Even the lack of an effect—sometimes called a *zero numerator*—can be a trap. Say someone reports, "We have treated 14 leukemic boys for five years with no resulting testicular dysfunction"—that is, zero abnormalities in 14. The question remains, How many cases would they have had to treat to have any real chance of seeing an effect?

The probability of an effect may be small yet highly important to know about.

All this means you must often ask: What's your *denominator*? What's the size of your population?** A disease rate of 10 percent in 20 individuals may not mean much. A 10 percent rate in 200 persons would be more impressive. A rate is only a figure. Always try to get both the numerator and the denominator.

The most important rule of all about any numbers: Ask for them. When anyone makes an assertion that should include numbers and fails to give them, when anyone says that most people, or even X percent, do such and such, you should ask: What are your numbers? After all, some researchers reportedly announced a new treatment for a disease of chickens by saying, "33.3 percent were cured, 33.3 percent died, and the other one got away."

Eliminate Bias; Consider Alternate Explanations

One scientist once said that lefties are overrepresented among baseball's heavy hitters. He saw this as "a possible result of their hemispheric lateralization, the relative roles of the two sides of the brain." A critic who had seen more ball games said some simpler covariables could explain the difference. When they swing, left-handed hitters are already on the move toward first base. And most pitchers are right-handers who throw most often to right-handed hitters.[14]

Scientist A was apparently guilty of *bias*, which in science means the introduction of spurious associations and error by failing to consider other factors that might influence the outcome. The other factors may be called covariables, covariates, intervening or contributing variables, confounding variables, or confounders. In simpler terms, this means "other explanations."

Statisticians call bias "the most serious and pervasive problem in the interpretation of data from clinical trials" ... "the central issue of epidemiological research" ... "the most common cause of unreliable data." Able and conscientious scientists try to eliminate biases or account for them in some way. But not everybody who makes a scientific, medical, or environmental claim is that skilled. Or that honest. Or that all-powerful. Some biases are unavoidable by the very difficulty of much research, and the most insidious biases of all, says one statistician, are "those we don't know exist."

A statistician recalled: "I was once called about a person who had won first, second, and third prizes in a church lottery. I was asked to assess the probability that this could have happened. I found out that the winner had bought nearly all the tickets." The statistician had of course asked the key question for both scientist and reporters: Could the relationship described be explained by other factors?

But bias is a pervasive human failing, and its effects often are more difficult to pin down. As one candid scientist is said to have admitted, "I wouldn't have seen it if I hadn't believed it."

Enthusiastic investigators often tell us their findings are exciting, and enthusiasm can be a good trait for scientists. But the findings may be so exciting that the investigators paint the results in over-rosy hues, forgetting needed caveats.

Other powerful human drives—the race for academic promotion and prestige, financial connections, other things—can also create conscious or unconscious attitudes that feed bias.

Two examples of where bias in the everyday-life meaning of the term may creep in:

Potential conflict of interest—Dr. Thomas Chalmers at Mount Sinai Medical Center in New York contrasts two drug trials, each sponsored by a pharmaceutical firm. In the first, the head of the study committee and the main statisticians and analysts were the firm's employees, though not so identified in any credits. In the second, the contract specifically called for a study protocol designed by independent investigators, and monitored by an outside board less likely to be influenced by a desire for a favorable outcome.

"It is never possible to eliminate" potential conflicts of interest in biomedical research, he concludes, but they should be disclosed so others can evaluate them.[15]

Finding what you expect to find, even if it's wrong— For years technicians making blood counts were guided by textbooks that told them two or more "properly" studied samples from the same blood should not vary beyond narrow "allowable" limits. Reported counts always stayed inside those limits. A Mayo Clinic statistician rechecked and found that at least two-thirds of the time the discrepancies exceeded the supposed limits. The technicians had been seeing what they had been told to expect, and discounting any differences as their mistakes. This also saved them from the additional labor of doing still more counting.

We add to our watch-out-for list:

The healthy-worker effect—Occupational studies often confront a seeming paradox: The workers exposed to some possible adverse effect turn out to be healthier than a control group of persons without such exposure. The confounder: the well-known *healthy-worker effect.* Workers tend to be healthier and live longer than the population in general. The simple reason: They normally have to be healthy to get their jobs in the first place, and then they must stay relatively healthy to keep their jobs. The healthy-worker effect can mislead you into thinking a workplace is safer than it really is.

The placebo effect and related phenomena—Both the *biased observer* and the *biased subject* are common in medicine. A researcher who wants to see a treatment result may see one. A patient may report one out of eagerness to please the researcher. There is also the powerful *placebo effect*. Summarizing many studies, one scientist found that half the patients with headaches or seasickness—and a third of those with coughs, mood changes, anxiety, the common cold, and even the disabling chest pains of angina pectoris—reported relief from a "nothing pill."[16]

A placebo is not truly a nothing pill. The mere expectation of relief seems to trigger important effects within the body. But in a careful study, the placebo should not do as well as a test medication. Otherwise the test medication is no better than a placebo.

Sampling bias—This can be a bugaboo of both political polls (see Chapter 10) and medical studies. Say you want to know what proportion of the populace has heart disease, so you stand on a corner and ask people as they pass. Your sample is biased, if only because it leaves out those too disabled to get around. Your problem, a statistician would say, is *selection*.[17]

Other examples: A doctor in a clinic or hospital with an unrepresentative patient population—healthier or sicker or richer or poorer than average—may report results that do not represent the population as a whole. Veterans Affairs (VA) hospitals, for example, treat relatively few women. Their conclusions may apply only to the disproportionate number of lower income men who typically seek out the VA hospitals' free care.

A celebrated Mayo or Cleveland or Ochsner clinic sees both a disproportionate number of difficult cases and a disproportionate number of patients who are affluent and well enough to travel.

Age and other key variables—Age, gender, occupation, nationality, race, income, socio-economic status, health status, and powerful behaviors such as smoking are all possible confounding—and frequently ignored—variables.

Four examples, each making a different point:

- *Exonerating a suspect*— In the 1970s, foes of adding fluoride to city water pointed to crude cancer mortality rates in 2 groups of 10 U.S. cities. One group had added fluoride to water, the other had not, and from 1950 to 1970 the cancer mortality rate rose faster in the fluoridated cities. The federal National Cancer Institute pointed out that the two groups were not equal: The difference in cancer deaths was almost entirely explained by differences in age, race, and gender. The age-, race-, and gender-adjusted difference actually showed a small, unexplained lower mortality rate in the fluoridated cities.[18]
- *Age or education?*—A 1947 survey of Chicago lawyers showed that those who had mere high school diplomas before entering legal training earned 6.3 percent more, on the average, than college graduates. The real explanation was age. In 1947 there were still many older lawyers without college degrees, and they were simply older, on the average, and hence more established.[19]
- *Occupation, race or some other factor?*—Some studies of workers in steel mills showed no overall increase in cancer, despite possible exposures to various carcinogens. But lumping all workers together can mask other important factors. It took a look at black workers alone to find excess cancer. They commonly worked at the coke ovens, where carcinogens were emitted. Such findings in blacks often may be falsely ascribed to race or genetics. The real or at least the most important contributing or ruling variables—to a statistician, the *independent variables*—may be occu-

pation and the social and economic plights that put blacks in vulnerable settings. The excess cancer is the *dependent variable*, the result.

"In a two-variable relationship," Dr. Gary Friedman explains, "one is usually considered the independent variable, which affects the other or dependent variable."[20]

• *Diseases with multiple causes*—We know that more people get colds in winter than at other times of the year. Weather is commonly seen as the underlying or independent variable, which affects the incidence of the common cold, the dependent variable. Actually, of course, some people, such as children in school who are constantly exposed to new viruses, are more vulnerable to colds than others. In the case of these children, then, there is often more than one independent variable.

Also, some people think that an important underlying reason for the prevalence of colds in winter may be that children are congregated in school, giving colds to each other, thence to their families, thence to their families' coworkers, thence to the coworkers' families, and so on. But cold weather and home heating may still figure, perhaps by drying nasal passages and making them more vulnerable to viruses.

The search for *true variables* is obviously one of the main pursuits of the epidemiologist, or disease detective—or of any physician who wants to know what has affected a patient, or of anyone who seeks true causes. Like colds, many medical conditions, such as heart disease, cancer, and probably mental illness, have multiple contributing factors.

Where many known, measurable factors are involved, statisticians can use mathematical techniques to relate all the variables and try to find which are the truly important predictors. The terms for this include multiple regression, multivariate analysis, and discriminant analysis and factor, cluster, path, and two-stage least-squares analyses.

Also remember: Smoking has been an important confounder in studies of industrial contaminants, in which the smokers suffer a disproportionate number of ill effects.[21]

Dropouts and other missing data—An investigator may also introduce bias by *constraining,* or distorting, a sample—by failing to reveal *nonresponse* or by otherwise "throwing away data."

Example: A surgeon cites his success rate in those discharged from the hospital after an operation but omits those who died during or just after the procedure.

Many people drop out of studies. Sometimes they just quit. Or they are dropped for various reasons: They could not be evaluated, they came down with some "irrelevant" disorders, they moved away, they died. In fact, many of those not counted may have had unfavorable outcomes had they stayed in the study.

The presence of significant nonresponse can often be detected, when reading medical papers, by counting the number of patients treated versus the number of untreated or differently treated controls—patients with whom the treated patients are compared. If the number of controls is strikingly greater in a randomized clinical trial (though not necessarily in an epidemiological or environmental study), there may have been many dropouts. A well-conducted study should describe and account for them. A study that does not may report a favorable treatment result by ignoring the fate of the dropouts.

Expect Variability

Regression toward the mean is the tendency of all values in every field of science—physical, biological, social, and economic—to move toward the average. Tall fathers tend to have shorter sons, and short fathers, taller sons. The students who get the highest grades on an exam tend to get somewhat lower ones the next time. The regression effect is common to all repeated measurements.

Regression is part of an even more basic phenomenon: *variation,* or *variability.* Virtually everything that is measured varies from measurement to measurement. When repeated, every experiment has at least slightly different results.

Examples: Take a patient's blood pressure, pulse rate, or blood count several times in a row, and the readings will be somewhat different. The important reasons? In part, fluctuating physiology, but also measurement errors, the limits of measurement accuracy, and observer variation. Examining the same patient, no two doctors will report exactly the same results, and the results may be very different.

If six doctors examine a patient with a faint heart murmur, only one or two may have the skill or keen hearing to detect it. Experimental results so typically differ from one time to the next that scientific and medical fakers—a Boston cancer researcher, for example—have been detected by the unusual regularity of their reported results. Their numbers agree too well and the same results appearing time after time, with not enough variation from patient to patient.

Biological variation is the most important cause of variation in physiology and medicine. Different patients, and the same patients, react differently to the same treatment. Disease rates differ in different parts of the country and among different populations, and—alas, nothing is simple— there is natural variation within the same population.

Every population, after all, is a collection of individuals, each with many characteristics. Each characteristic, or *variable,* such as height, has a *distribution* of values from person to person, and—if we would know something about the whole population—we must have some handy summaries of the distribution. We can't get much out of a list of 10,000 measurements, so we need single values that summarize many measurements.

Some important terms:

Averages and related measures—The *mean, median,* and *mode* can give us some idea of the look of the whole and its many measurable properties, or *parameters.*

When most of us speak of an average, we mean simply the *mean* or *arithmetic average,* the sum of all the values divided by the number of values. The mean is no mean tool; it is a good way to get a typical number, but it has limitations, especially when there are some extreme values.

Example: There is said to be a memorial in a Siberian town to a fictitious Count Smerdlovski, the world's champion at Russian roulette. On the average he won, but his actual record was 73 and 1.[22]

If you look at the arithmetic average of salaries in Company X, you will not know that a third of the personnel are working for the minimum wage, while a few make $100,000 or more a year. You may learn more here from the *median*— which is the midpoint in a list of figures. You also can think of the median as the middle value. In Company X, the median salary is $30,000 a year; half the employees earn that much or less, and the other half earn that much or more.

The median can be of value when a group has a few members with extreme values, like the 400-pounder at an obesity clinic whose other patients weigh from 180 to 200 pounds. If he leaves, the patients' mean weight might drop by 10 pounds, but the median might drop just 1 pound.[23]

The most frequently occurring number or value in a distribution is called the *mode.* When the median and the mode are about the same, or even more when mean, median, and mode are roughly equal, you can feel comfortable about knowing the typical value. When plotted on a graph, this is a *bell curve.*

With many of the things that scientists, economists, or others measure and then plot on a graph—test scores are just examples—we typically tend to see a familiar, bell-shaped *normal distribution,* high in the middle and low at each end, or *tail.* This bell curve is also called a *Gaussian curve,* named after the 19th century German mathematician Karl Friedrich Gauss.

But you may also find that the plot has two or more peaks or clusters, a *bimodal* or *multimodal distribution.*

Range and distribution—You still need to know something about the exceptions, in short, the *dispersion* (or spread or scatter) of the entire distribution. One measure of spread is the *range.* It tells you the lowest and highest values. It might inform you, for example, that the annual salaries in a company range from $10,000 to $250,000.

You can also divide your values into 100 *percentiles,* so you can say someone or something falls into the 10th or 71st percentile, or into *quartiles* (fourths) or *quintiles* (fifths). One useful measure is the *interquartile range,* the interval between the 75th and 25th percentiles—this is the distribution in the middle, which avoids the extreme values at each end. Or you can divide a distribution into subgroups—those with incomes from $10,000 to $20,000, for example, or ages 20 to 29, 30 to 39, and so on.

Standard deviation—A widely used number, the *standard deviation,* can reveal a great deal. No matter how it sounds, it is not the average distance from the mean but a more complex figure. Unlike the range, this handy figure takes full account of every value to tell how spread out things are—how dispersed the measurements.

Here's what one statistician calls a truly remarkable generalization: In most sets of measurement "and without regard to what is being measured," only 1 measurement in 3 will deviate from the average by more than 1 standard deviation, only 1 in 20 by more than 2 standard deviations, and only 1 in 100 by more than 2.57 standard deviations.

"Once you know the standard deviation in a normal, bell-shaped distribution," according to the University of Minnesota's Thomas Louis, "you can draw the whole picture of the data. You can visualize the shape of the curve without even drawing the picture, since the larger the variation of the numbers, the larger the standard deviation and the more spread out the curve—and vice versa."

Example: If the average score of all students who take the SAT college entrance test is relatively low and the spread—the standard deviation—is relatively large, this creates a very long-tailed, low-humped curve of test scores, ranging, say, from around 300 to 1500. But if the average score of a group of brighter students entering an elite college is high, the standard deviation of the scores will be less and the curve will be high-humped and short-tailed, going from maybe 900 to 1500.

"If I just told you the means of two such distributions, you might say they were the same," another scientist says. "But if I reported the means and the standard deviations, you'd know they were different, with a lot more variations in one."

Putting a Human Face on Variability

From a human standpoint, variation tells us that it takes more than averages to describe individuals. Biologist Stephen Jay Gould learned in 1982 that he had a serious form of cancer. The literature told him the median survival was only eight months after discovery. Three years later he wrote in *Discover*, "All evolutionary biologists know that means and medians are the abstractions," while variation is "the reality," meaning "half the people will live longer" than eight months.

Since he was young, since his disease had been diagnosed early, and since he would receive the best possible treatment, he decided he had a good chance of being at the far end of the curve. He calculated that the curve must be skewed well to the right, as the left half of the distribution had to be "scrunched up between zero and eight months, but the upper right half [could] extend out for years."

He concluded, "I saw no reason why I shouldn't be in that small tail. . . . I would have time to think, to plan and to fight." Also, since he was being placed on an experimental new treatment, he might if fortune smiled "be in the first cohort of a new distribution with . . . a right tail extending to death by natural causes at advanced old age."[24]

In 1999, Gould became president of the American Association for the Advancement of Science, the world's largest membership organization representing all scientific disciplines.

Statistics cannot tell us whether fortune will smile, only that such reasoning is sound.

What's a Good Study?

4

Why think? Why not try an experiment?

—John Hunter, 18th century British anatomist

Sit down before fact as a little child, be prepared to give up every preconceived notion, follow humbly wherever and to whatever abysses nature leads, or you shall learn nothing.

—Thomas Henry Huxley

This is the part I always hate.

—A mathematician as he approaches the equal sign
(in a Sidney Harris cartoon in *American Scientist*)

$\mathcal{E}$ $\mathcal{E}$ $\mathcal{E}$

The big problems of statistics, say its best practitioners, have little to do with computations and formulas. They have to do with judgment—how to design a study, how to conduct it, then how to analyze and interpret the results. Journalism, with many chances to do harm by shaky reporting, also calls for sophisticated judgment. How, then, can we tell which studies seem credible, which we should report?

Different problems require different methods, different numbers. One of the most basic questions in science is: Is the study designed in a way that will allow the researchers to answer the questions that they want answered?

We'll start with two case histories. The first comes from a clinical study of a drug, the other from an epidemiological study of a disease outbreak. The first led to unfounded hopes. The second is a short detective story with a surprise ending.

Case study 1: Physicians at a prestigious New England university used catheters to slowly infuse a theoretically promising drug into the skulls of four Alzheimer's patients. According to the patients' families, three of the patients improved and the fourth at least held his own.

The university held a news conference, with one of the patients brought forth for an on-camera testimonial. The researcher used some cautious words, but some newspaper headlines didn't. The story flew far and wide. The medical center got 2,600 phone calls, mainly from families of Alzheimer's patients who were desperate for any glimmer of hope.

There are two big reasons to question this study. A study of just four patients usually means little. A study whose effectiveness is judged by desperate family members is highly suspect. Further study found that the drug didn't work.

Of course, many good studies are responsible for the many, many drugs and other new treatments that have revolutionized medicine and saved countless lives.

But in the four-patient Alzheimer's study, Harvard's Dr. Jay Winsten concluded, "The visual impact of [one] patient's on-camera testimonials all but guaranteed that TV coverage would oversell the research, despite any qualifying language."[1]

Case study 2: Minnesota Department of Health epidemiologists investigated a large outbreak of hepatitis A at a county club outing in 1978. They interviewed many of the more than 100 people who had become ill after eating at the club and, for comparison purposes, some who ate there but hadn't become ill.

This case-control study discovered a strong statistical association between eating hot dogs and becoming ill. But wait a minute! The cooking of the hot dog meat should have killed the hepatitis virus.

The problem turned out *not* to be the hot dogs as served. But the study had put the epidemiologists on the right track. Lab tests found the virus in the relish that people put on their hot dogs.

Further study discovered that a food worker who was handling the relish carried the hepatitis A virus. He found other work until he no longer was infectious. The cases of hepatitis stopped.[2] More about the great benefits, as well as limits, of case-control studies in a moment.

Epidemiology has its problems and controversies along with its many, many successes. The cause or causes of Gulf War Syndrome still stir debate, for example. And while epidemiologists led the way in showing preventative strategies for AIDS, some critics charged that progress was slow at the start of that epidemic.

Together, clinical trials (also called clinical studies or patient trials) and epidemiological studies cover virtually the entire spectrum of health care.

Clinical trials evaluate drugs, other treatments, vaccines and diagnostic procedures by testing them in humans, to see what will work and what won't.

Epidemiological studies probe the patterns and causes of all sorts of diseases and other health risks. These studies seek the answers that can prevent or limit future cases, so that we can live longer, healthier lives.

Before getting to the details of clinical and epidemiological studies, let's step back for a broader view and some history.

Experiments versus Seductive Anecdotes

Scientific evidence can be weighed according to what's been called a hierarchy of evidence. Some kinds of studies carry more weight than others.

Science and medicine started with anecdotes, unreliable as far as generalization is concerned, yet provocative. Anecdotes matured into systematic observation. Observation told the ancients much about the stars, and it is still important today. Simple eyeballing has developed into data collection and the recording of case histories. These are indispensable methods, yet still only one part of science. Case histories may not be typical, or they may reflect the beholder. Medicine continues to be plagued by big authorities who insist, "I know what I see."

There can still be useful, even inspired, observation and analysis of *natural experiments*. Excess fluoride in some waters hardened teeth, and this observation provided the first clue that fluoridation of drinking water might prevent tooth decay.

In 1585 or so, Galileo dropped weights from a tower and helped invent the *scientific experiment*. This means a study in which the experimenter controls the conditions and records the effect. Experiments on objects, animals, germs, and people matured into the modern experimental study, in which the experimenter changes only one thing, or some precisely planned number of things, to see how this affects the outcome.

It's a step-by-step process that, when done right, is done with care. Take a new potential treatment. Typically, the research starts in laboratory dishes or other lab apparatus, where it's relatively easy (and safe) to make changes. Then the research, if promising, may progress to animal trials (see Chapter 6). Yes, we must question whether specific lab and animal findings apply to humans. Those questions can only be answered if the research progresses to, and then passes, the next step: clinical trials— that is, trials in people.*

At each step along this way, all conscientious studies have one guiding principle: Each has a careful *design*. That is, it has the method or plan of attack that includes the right kind and number of patients or animals or petri dishes, and it tries to eliminate bias. Different kinds of studies require different methods. So one of the basic questions for a researcher is: Can this kind of experiment, this design, yield the answers I seek?

Clinical Researchers at Work

Experimental medicine's "gold standard" is the controlled, randomized clinical trial.[3] At its best, the investigator tests a treatment or drug or some other intervention by randomly selecting at least two comparable groups of people, the *experimental group* that is tested or treated and a *control group* that is observed for comparison.

Good clinical trials are expensive and difficult. It has been estimated that of 100 scheduled trials, 60 are abandoned, not implemented, or not completed. This may be for lack of funds, difficulty in recruiting or keeping patients, toxicity or other problems, or, sometimes, rapid evidence of a difference in effect (making continued denial of effective treatment to patients in a control group unethical). Another 20 trials produce no noteworthy results, and just 20 have results worth publishing.

A few of many possible examples: Randomized clinical trials proved that new drugs could cut the heart attack death rate, that treating hypertension could prevent strokes, and that polio, measles, and hepatitis vaccines worked. No doctor, observing a limited number of patients, could have shown these things.

Types of studies—Clinical studies can be classified by how a treatment is evaluated:

- Among the most reliable are *parallel studies* comparing similar groups given different treatments, or a treatment versus no treatment. But such studies are not always possible.
- In *crossover studies* the same patients get two or more treatments in succession and act as their own controls. Similarly, *self-controlled studies* evaluate an experimental treatment by controlled observations during periods of no treatment or of some standard treatment.

There are potential pitfalls here. Treatment A might affect the outcome of treatment B, despite the usual use of a washout period between study periods. Patients become acclimated: They may become more tolerant of pain or side effects or, now more health-conscious, may change their ways.

The patients in a control group don't always behave in parallel studies either. In one large-scale trial of methods to lower blood cholesterol and the risk of heart disease, many controls adopted some of the same methods—quitting cigarette smoking, eating fewer fats—and reduced their risk too.

- Investigators often use *historical controls,* which means comparison with old records. Historically the cure rate has been 30 percent, say, and the new therapy cures 60 percent. Or researchers use other *external controls* (such as comparison with other studies). These controls are often misleading. The groups compared aren't always comparable. The treatments may have been given by different methods. But this approach is still at times useful.

Historical controls often are used for nonclinical studies too. *Examples:* Researchers want to see the effect of an increase in cigarette taxes on smokers; the researchers compare smoking rates and cigarette sales before and after the tax increase. Researchers want to look at the effect of lowering the highway speed limit; they compare before and after accident rates. But always ask: Were there any other changes that might have affected the smoking rates, the accident rate, or whatever is being studied?

Clinical Studies: How to Judge Them

All studies, including the best, have potential pitfalls. Here's a look at what makes clinical studies—and in some cases other types of studies too—as good as they can be:

1. Adequate controls are needed if you want to put the results in the bank.

2. The number of patients must be large enough, whether 10 or 10,000, to get trustworthy results, and representative enough so the findings will apply to a larger population. Because people vary so widely in their reactions, and a few patients can fool you, fair-sized groups of patients are usually needed. Picking patients for a medical study is similar to picking citizens to be questioned in a political poll. In both, a sample is studied and inferences— the outcome of an election, the results in patients in general—are made for a larger population.

To get a large enough sample, medical researchers can conduct *multicenter trials*. Such trials are appealing because they can include hundreds of patients, but expensive and tricky because one must try to maintain similar selection and quality control at 10 institutions, maybe even 100 institutions. This approach also helps guard against institutional or regional bias. Successful multicenter trials established the value of controlling hypertension to prevent strokes and demonstrated the strong probability that less extensive surgery is as effective as more drastic surgery for many breast cancer patients.

3. The patients should be randomized, that is, divided by some random method into experimental and control groups. Randomization can easily be violated. A doctor assigning patients to treatment A or B may, seeing a particular type of patient, say or think, "This patient will be better on B."

If treatment B has been established as better than A, there should be no random study in the first place and certainly no study of that doctor's patient. When randomization is violated, "the trial's guarantee of lack of bias goes down the drain," says one critique. As a result, patients who consent to randomization are often assigned to study groups according to a list of computer-generated random numbers.

4. "Blinding" can add much confidence to a study. To combat bias in investigators or patients, studies should be blinded. To the extent feasible, they can be single-, double-, or, best of all, triple-blinded—so that neither the doctors nor the nurses administering a treatment, nor the patients, nor those who assess the results know whether today's pill is treatment A, treatment B, or an ineffective placebo. Otherwise, a doctor or patient who yearns for a good result may see or feel one when the "right" drug is given. There is a tale of an overzealous receptionist who, knowing which patients were getting the real drug and not the placebo, was so encouraging to these patients that they began saying they felt good willy-nilly.[4]

Barring observant receptionists, the use of a placebo—from the Latin "I shall please"—may help maintain "blindness." Placebos actually give some relief in a third of all patients, on the average, in various conditions. The effect is usually temporary, however, and a truly effective drug ought to work substantially better than the placebo.

Blinding is often impossible or unwise. Some treatments don't lend themselves to it, particularly many types of surgery. And some drugs quickly reveal themselves by various effects. But an unblinded test is a weaker test.

5. The research findings need to be stratified, to test them and to discover the most from them. That is, for analysis they are separated into groups by age, gender, socio-economic status, and so on. This can combat the influence of confounding variables and can get answers applicable to various populations. Failure to stratify can hide true associations in various types of studies.

An example from a clinical study: A study of open-heart surgery patients may separate out those who had to wait for their surgery. Some patients die waiting; those left are relatively stronger patients who do better, on average, than those treated immediately after diagnosis.

An example from epidemiology: The role of high-absorbency tampons in toxic shock syndrome was clarified only when the cases were broken down by the precise types of tampon used. More about that in a moment.

An example from economics: Even in times of high employment, breakdowns by age and race might show problem pockets of joblessness.

Large studies are generally necessary for stratification. When researchers subdivide their findings, the numbers in each subgroup get smaller. If the subgroups are too small, a finding may be missed.

6. A good study is reported fairly and candidly by the research team. Dr. John Bailar warns of practices that sometimes have much value but at other times are "inappropriate and improper and, to the extent that they are deceptive, unethical." Among them: The selective reporting of findings, leaving out some that might not fit the conclusion. The reporting of a single study in multiple fragments, when the whole might not sound so good. And the failure to report the low power of some studies, their inability to detect a result even if one existed.[5]

Alternative Medicine

Alternative (sometimes called complementary) medicine can involve herbal medications, a variety of stress-reduction techniques, acupuncture, and various other unconventional approaches. Some alternative approaches have been shown to help. More and more studies are being done to assess which others may help and which may not. What standards should we use to judge these approaches?

Our belief: Alternative medicine and conventional medicine should be judged by the same standards. Both affect our bodies and our pocketbooks.

"Disease Detectives" at Work

In earlier times, epidemiology was concerned wholly with epidemics like smallpox, typhoid, and other infections. In 1740 Percival Pott scored a famous epidemiological success by observing the high rate of scrotum cancer in London's chimney sweeps. He correctly blamed it on their exposure to soot-burned organic material, much like a smoked cigarette. A century later, John Snow, plotting London cholera cases on a map and noting a cluster around one source of drinking water, removed the handle from the now famed Broad Street pump and helped end a deadly epidemic.

In today's world of drug abuse and road rage, epidemics are no longer limited to diseases. The mandate of disease detectives—formally called epidemiologists—has widened to meet the new challenges.

Today, "Epidemiology cuts across all aspects of health and behavior, it involves all aspects of public health," said Dr. Michael Osterholm, former state epidemiologist for Minnesota, now chairman and CEO of Infection Control Advisory Network, Inc. (ican, inc.), in Eden Prairie, Minnesota.

Today's epidemiologists still track down infectious diseases. They have found the causes of new scourges, such as toxic shock syndrome, Legionnaires' disease, and AIDS. And they probe outbreaks of many old as well as some new illnesses, promoting prevention when the way is known, and always trying to learn more.

Today's epidemiologists also study noninfectious diseases, which have become the biggest killers in our modern world. Epidemiologists successfully indicted smoking as a cause of lung cancer and heart disease. They identified the association of fats and cholesterol with clogging of the heart's arteries, changing the way that most

Americans eat. And they pointed the way to the nation's exercise boom as a way of improving health.

They also provide the human-toll figures and other evidence that stir political debates over issues ranging from gun control to buckling-up in your car. They study everything from environmental problems to the effects of stress, from child and maternal health to the problems of aging.

In all these many ways considered together, epidemiologists may affect how we live our lives more than any other scientists.

Just as with clinical studies, epidemiological studies follow the basic rules of scientific and statistical analysis described in earlier chapters. And just as with clinical studies, epidemiological studies can take different forms to tackle different questions.

All forms of epidemiological studies have value, and all have limits. All look for telltale patterns that can reveal the causes of health-related problems. All seek preventive approaches or other strategies for better health.

Epidemiology, like all science, started with *observational studies,* and these remain important. These studies, without comparison groups, are uncertain when it comes to determining cause and effect. Yet observation is how we first learned of the unfortunate effects of toxic rain, Agent Orange, cigarette smoking, and many sometimes helpful, sometimes harmful medications.

Types of studies—Some observational studies are simply *descriptive*—describing the incidence, prevalence, and mortality rates of various diseases, for example. Other, *analytic* studies seek to analyze or explain: The Seven-Country Study, for example, helped associate high meat and dairy fat and cholesterol consumption with excess risk of coronary heart disease.

Ecological studies look for links between environmental conditions and illness.

Human migrations such as the Japanese who came to the United States, ate more fat, and developed more disease are *natural experiments.*

Many epidemiological surveys rely on *samples* to represent the whole. These include government surveys of health and nutritional habits, of driving patterns and drug abuse. Samples and surveys often use questionnaires to get information. Questionnaires can be no better than the quality of the answers.

Example: One survey compared patients' reporting of their current chronic illnesses with those their doctors recorded. The patients failed to mention almost half of the conditions the doctors detected over the course of a year.

Whether it comes to illness, diets, or drinking, people tend to put themselves in the best possible light. A survey may stand or fall on the use of sophisticated ways to get accurate information. (See Chapter 10 on polling techniques.)

Epidemiologists' studies may also be classified in other ways:

- A *prevalence study* is a wide-angle snapshot of a population. It's a look at the rate of disease X or health-related problem Z, and its possible effects by age, gender, or other variables. This also may be called a current or cross-sectional study.
- A *case-control study* examines cases, along with a control group, for an intense, close-up analysis of a disease's relationship to other factors. The case-control study is a great way to assemble clues, to focus the investigation. But more research often must follow to nail down the culprit. A good example is the hot dogs and relish case at the beginning of this chapter.

Other examples: The nation hears of cases of toxic shock syndrome, mainly in young women. Epidemiologists at the federal Centers for Disease Control and Prevention launch a field investigation to find a series of patients, or cases. The epidemiologists confirm the diagnosis, then interview the patients and their families and other contacts to assemble careful case histories that cover, hopefully, all possible causes or associations. This group is then compared with a randomly selected matched comparison (control) group of healthy young women of like age and other characteristics. The women who developed toxic shock were much more likely to have used tampons. But it took more study, by Osterholm and others, to show that the real risk was in high-absorbency tampons.

The relationship of cigarette smoking to lung cancer, the association of birth control pills with blood vessel problems, and the transmission patterns of AIDS all were identified in case-control studies that pointed the way for detailed, confirming investigations.

- *Cohort* or *incidence studies* are motion pictures. Researchers pick a group of people, or cohort (a cohort was a unit of a Roman legion). Then the researchers follow the people in the cohort over time, often for years, to see how some disease or diseases develop. These studies are costly and difficult. Subjects drop out or disappear. Large numbers must be studied to see rare events.

But cohort studies can be powerful instruments, and can substitute for randomized experiments that would be ethically impossible. You can't ethically expose a group to an agent that you suspect would cause a disease. You can watch a group so exposed.

Examples: The noted Framingham study of ways of life that might be associated with developing heart disease has followed more than 5,000 residents of that Massachusetts town since 1948. The American Cancer Society's 1952–55 study of 187,783 men aged 50 to 69, with 11,780 of them dying during that period, did much to establish that cigarette smoking was strongly associated with developing lung cancer.[6]

Another way of classification, for both epidemiological and clinical studies, involves timing:

- *Retrospective* studies look back in time—at medical records, vital statistics, or people's recollections. People who have a disease are questioned to try to find common habits or exposures. Possible limitations to watch for: Memories may play tricks. Old records may be poor and misleading. Definitions of diseases and methods of diagnosis vary over the years.
- *Prospective* studies, like the Framingham and the American Cancer Society studies, look forward. They focus sharply on a selected group who are all followed by the same statistical and medical techniques.

Dr. Eugene Robin at Stanford tells how four separate retrospective clinical studies affirmed the accuracy of a test for blood clots in the lungs. When an adequate prospective clinical trial was done, most of the retrospective looks were proved wrong.[7]

Finally, *intervention* studies involve doing something to some of the subjects. The massive, hugely successful 1954 field trial of the Salk polio vaccine was a classic epidemiological intervention study—and a clinical trial too.[8] Another successful intervention study, a community trial, established the value of fluoridating water supplies to prevent tooth decay. Some towns had their water fluoridated; some did not. Blinding was impossible, but the striking difference in dental cavities that resulted could not have been caused by any placebo effect.

Disease Outbreaks:
What to Watch For

Epidemiologists study and act on other worrisome outbreaks that pop up regularly across the nation. These include serious respiratory ailments, various food-borne illnesses (with life-threatening E. coli just one example), and meningitis. They include the surprise outbreak of an African strain of life-threatening encephalitis that appeared in New York City in 1999, and all sorts of other diseases. And these disease detectives—just like police detectives—sometimes must move early, issuing warnings and alerts when very little evidence is in.

Dr. Michael Osterholm listed five things that reporters should keep in mind as they deal with the numbers while covering disease outbreaks:

1. Common symptoms can inflate numbers. When health officials investigate a food-borne outbreak, they can't assume that everyone who reports having symptoms actually has that illness.

Diarrhea and gastrointestinal cramps are common and can be caused by a variety of things. Headaches and stiff necks can be caused by many things, not necessarily meningitis. Fever and aches can be caused by many things, not necessarily some new strain of influenza that's in the news. Legionnaires' disease can be confused with common forms of pneumonia.

Health officials investigating an outbreak may classify cases into three groups: possible, probable, and confirmed. Reporters should report this and ask: How are you deciding which cases are in each group? Are lab tests needed to confirm the diagnosis?

2. An increase in reported cases may be due to more reporting, not more actual cases. When there are a lot of news reports about Lyme disease, food-borne outbreaks, and many other illnesses, more people are likely to see their doctors or phone public health agencies. Reported-case totals rise. Just as many cases may have been *occurring* before the news reports, although many were not being *reported.*

3. What appears to be one big outbreak may be several mini-outbreaks. Fortunately, epidemiologists have an important new lab technique; "genetic fingerprinting" often can tell them whether scattered cases of an infectious illness are related.

Example offered by Osterholm: An increased number of hepatitis A cases are being reported in a large metropolitan area. "Genetic fingerprinting" may show that the virus strains from all the cases are precisely the same, pointing to a single source of the outbreak. *Or* this new type of lab test may show slight variations in the strains involved. Further study then may find that some of the cases started in a day-care center, some started with an infected food-handler, and some were introduced by a foreign traveler.

So if there are scattered cases of some illnesses in your community with no clear link, ask: Has your lab done "genetic fingerprinting" to see if all the cases are really connected?

4. When there's a national problem, check the numbers to see what's happening in your community.

Example: The nation's AIDS epidemic started with cases reported in California and New York. The virus got a chance to spread in those states before the peril was clearly recognized; for various reasons, the spread to and within other states has been uneven. The rate of AIDS cases (per 100,000 population) is about 40 times higher in New York than in North

Dakota. Even within a state, there often are big differences between metropolitan and rural areas.[9]

Other disease patterns vary from region to region, for a variety of reasons. All this may require different prevention priorities in different geographical areas, and different reporting by journalists.

5. When controversy flares, don't be surprised to find that the true numbers are in the middle.

Again an *example* from AIDS: Early in this epidemic, some nonexperts predicted that AIDS would spread widely through the heterosexual community. Others took the opposite extreme, saying this virus could not be spread through vaginal intercourse. It's now clear that the large majority of AIDS cases in the United States have been in gay men and in needle-sharing drug abusers. But some cases do occur when infected people (needle-using drug abusers, bisexual men, prostitutes, etc.) spread the virus to their heterosexual partners.

Epidemiological studies do have their limitations. They can link cigarette smoking to various types of cancer. But laboratory studies are needed to pin down just how smoking causes the cellular changes that spell malignancy. Epidemiological studies can show how a new type of virus is spreading and which parts of the population are most vulnerable. But laboratory studies and then clinical studies are needed to find a treatment or vaccine.

Despite this, the preventive messages that typically come out of epidemiological studies can be vitally important. For example, "epi studies" (as they often are called) allowed the nation to take steps to limit the spread of AIDS before the virus that causes this illness was even discovered.

Even limited knowledge sometimes can go a long way in public health.

Example: Reye Syndrome is a life-threatening brain disorder that typically occurs (a) only in children, (b) after they've had either chicken pox or influenza, and (c) if they took aspirin. Even then, only some children developed Reye, far from all.[10] To this day, experts aren't sure how these factors can come together to trigger Reye Syndrome, Osterholm noted. But after national epidemiological studies gathered the numbers that showed the aspirin-Reye link, warnings were issued. Parents paid heed. Moms and dads stopped using aspirin to treat flu-like illnesses in children, switching to other pain relievers. The number of Reye cases dropped dramatically.

The mothers and fathers didn't need to wait for laboratory scientists to discover the specific way that aspirin can combine with other factors to cause Reye Syndrome. Similarly, back in 1854, John Snow didn't know what germ caused cholera when he pulled the London pump handle that stopped that epidemic.

Checklist—See "Reporting a Disease Outbreak" in the Appendix for questions that reporters can ask when covering a disease outbreak.

Questions You Can Ask

5

Just because Dr. Famous or Dr. Bigshot says this is what he found doesn't mean it is necessarily so.

—Dr. Arnold Relman

Ask to see the numbers, not just the pretty colors.

—Dr. Richard Margolin, National Institutes of Health, describing PET scans to reporters

Good questions can be golden.

One of this book's authors (Cohn) once asked Dr. Morris Fishbein, the provocative genius who long edited the *Journal of the American Medical Association*, "How can I, a reporter, tell whether a doctor is doing a good job of caring for his patients?" Fishbein immediately replied, "Ask him how often he has a patient take off his shirt."

His lesson was plain: No physical exam is complete unless the patient takes off his or her clothes.

Two other examples of golden questions with broad applications:

- Early in 1999, researchers reported on a big dietary study, involving about 89,000 women. Their key conclusion was that fiber in the diet doesn't lower the risk of colon cancer. *Time* magazine's Christine Gorman probed deeper for a bigger picture.

The result: The magazine's headline read "Still High on Fiber." While fiber may not protect against colon cancer, other studies provide strong evidence that it is "good for your heart" and helps to keep your body healthy in other ways, Gorman informed her readers.[1]

The lesson: Always ask yourself, and ask others as necessary, "Do I have the full picture?"

• Some top science reporters make it a habit to ask experts, at the end of an interview, "What question should I have asked, but didn't?"

The interviewer gets a last crack at getting answers to questions that he or she forgot to ask. The person being interviewed often appreciates the chance to say something that she or he has been thinking about. And gems often fall out of this final exchange.

In Chapter 3 we suggested that you ask researchers these basic questions about their conclusions or claims: How do you know? Have you (or others) done a study or any experiments? If so, were they acceptable ones, by general agreement? Were they without any substantial bias? Are the conclusions backed by believable statistical evidence? And what is the degree of certainty or uncertainty? How sure can you be?

And to put the study in perspective: Are your results fairly consistent with those from any related studies, and with general knowledge in the field? Have the findings resulted in a consensus among other experts in the field?

In some cases there may be no studies at all, only anecdotal information that raises some concern. "There are four cases in our block" may be worth investigating, maybe worth even a cautious news story, but there is not yet anything close to certainty.

Assuming there has been a study, a researcher's scientific presentation may answer all of these questions to your satisfaction. In fact, if you must ask too many questions, that in itself might hint that the study is lacking in some regard. But some studies, some claims, some controversies require you to probe deeper. You may need to focus on one specific area, or several. You may want to carry the story to the next journalistic step: What now?

Don't be reticent about asking what you need to know. You're just following the path of good science.

A properly skeptical scientist, starting a study, may begin with a *null hypothesis*—that a new treatment *won't* work. Then the scientist sees whether or not the evidence disproves the null hypothesis—and, in doing so, proves that there is statistically significant evidence that the new treatment really works.

This approach is much like the law's presumption of innocence. It is for the prosecutor to prove beyond reasonable doubt that the suspect is guilty. A reporter, without being cynical, should be equally skeptical and greet every claim by saying, in words or thought, "Show me."

This chapter is a smorgasbord of questions. Like any good smorgasbord, pick and choose what you want and need. And, of course, you can fashion questions of your own.

1. Is the study large enough to pass statistical muster?

How many subjects (patients, cases, other people, etc.) are you talking about? Are these numbers large enough, statistically rigorous enough, to get the answers you want? Was there an adequate number of patients to show a difference between treatments?

Small numbers can sometimes carry weight. "Sometimes small samples are the best we can do," one researcher says. But larger numbers are always more likely to pass statistical muster.

The number can depend on the situation. A thorough physiological study of five cases of some difficult disorder may be important. One new case of smallpox would be a shocker in a world in which smallpox has supposedly been eliminated. In June 1981 the federal Centers for Disease Control and Prevention reported that five young men, all active homosexuals, had been treated for *Pneumocystis carinii* pneumonia at three Los Angeles hospitals.[2] This alerted the world to what became the AIDS epidemic.

P **(for probability) value**—Could your results have occurred just by chance? Have any statistical tests been applied to test this?

Did you calculate a *P* value? Was it favorable—.05 or less? *P* values and confidence statements need not be regarded as straitjackets, but like jury verdicts, they indicate reasonable doubt or reasonable certainty.

Remember that positive findings are more likely to be reported and published than negative findings. Remember that a favorable-sounding *P* value of .05 means only that there is just 1 chance in 20, or a 5 percent probability, that the statistics could have come out this way by pure chance when there was actually no effect.

There are ways and ways of arriving at *P* values. For example, an investigator may choose to report one of several end points: death, length of survival, blood pressure, other measurements, or just the patient's condition on leaving the hospital. All can be important, but a *P* value can be misleading if the wrong one is picked or emphasized.

You might ask yourself: How important is hospital discharge if many of the patients die within a few days after returning home?

A general question you might ask researchers: Did you collaborate with a statistician in both your design and your analysis?

2. Is the study designed well? Could unintentional bias have affected the results?

Type and design of study—What kind of study was it? Do you think it was the right kind of study to get the answer you sought?

Was there a systematic research plan or design? And a *protocol* (a set of rules for the study)? Was the design drawn before you started your study? What specific questions or hypotheses did you set out to test or answer? Why did you do it that way?

If an investigator patiently tells you about an acceptable-sounding design, that's worth a brownie point. If the answer is "Huh?" or a nasty one, that may tell you something else. See Chapter 4 for a discussion of study types and their uses and limits.

Patient selection—Who were your subjects? How were they selected? What were your criteria for admission to the study? Were rigorous laboratory tests used (if possible) to define the patients' diagnoses?

Was the assignment of subjects, to treatment or a comparison group, done on a random basis? Were the patients admitted to the study before the randomization? This helps eliminate bias.

If the subjects weren't randomized, why not? One statistician says, "If it is a non-randomized study, a biased investigator can get some extraordinary results by carefully picking his subjects."

Control group—Was there a control or comparison group? If not, the study will be weaker. Who or what were your controls or bases for comparison? In other words: When you say you have such and such a result, what are you comparing it with? Are the study or patient group and the control group similar in all respects, except the treatment or other variable being studied?

Thomas M. Vogt calls "comparison of non-comparable groups probably . . . the single most common error in the medical and popular literature on health and disease."[3]

Representative?—Were your patients and controls representative of the general population? Or of a particular population—people with the disease or condition you are interested in?

The answers here go a long way toward answering these questions: To what populations are the results applicable? Would the association hold for other groups?

If your groups are not comparable to the general population or some important populations, have you taken steps to adjust for this? Have you used either statistical adjustment or stratification of your sample to find out about specific groups? Or both? Samples can be adjusted for age, for example, to make an older- or younger-than-average sample more nearly comparable to the general populace.

"Blinding" and quality control—Was the study blinded? In a study comparing drugs or other forms of treatment with a placebo or dummy treatment, did (1) those administering the treatment, (2) those getting it, and (3) those assessing the outcome know who was getting what? Or were they indeed blinded, and not know who was getting what?

Could those giving or getting the treatment have easily guessed which was which by a difference in reaction or taste or other results?

Not every study can be a blind study. One researcher says, "There can be ethical problems in not telling patients what drug they're taking and the possible side effects. People are not guinea pigs." True, but a blinded study will always carry more conviction.

Were there other accepted quality controls—for example, making sure (perhaps by counting pills or studying urine samples) that the patients supposed to take a pill really took it? Were you able to follow your study plan?

Surveys, questionnaires, interviews—Were the questions likely to elicit accurate, reliable answers? Respondents' answers can differ sharply, depending on how questions are asked.

Example: In one study 1,153 people were asked which is safer, a treatment that kills 10 percent of every 100 patients or a treatment with a 90 percent survival rate? More people voted for the second way of saying precisely the same thing.[4]

People commonly give inaccurate answers to sensitive questions, such as those about sexual behavior. They are notoriously inaccurate in reporting their own medical histories, even those of recent months. And they may fudge their answers when asked if they do things they know they should, such as using the car seatbelts.

Dropouts—How many of your study subjects completed the course? Do you account for those who dropped out and tell why they did?

Every study has dropouts. Dr. David Sackett at McMaster University says, "Patients do not disappear . . . for trivial reasons. Rather, they leave . . . because they refuse therapy, recover, die, or retire to the Sunbelt with their permanent disability."

If an investigator ignores those who didn't do well and dropped out, it can make the outcome look better. Sometimes those who died of "other causes" are listed among "survivors" of the disease being investigated. This is sometimes done on the theory that, after all, they didn't die of the target cause. But this can make a treatment look better than it really is, unless there are equal numbers of such deaths in every branch of the study.

Sackett adds, "The loss to follow-up of 10 percent of the original inception cohort is cause for concern. If 20 percent or more are not accounted for, the results . . . are probably not worth reading."[5] (Vogt comments on this: "Generally true, but utterly dependent on the situation.")

Potential conflict of interest—Ask, when appropriate: Where did the money to support the study come from? Many honest investigators are financed by companies that may profit from the outcome. All studies are financed by some source. In any case, the public should know any pertinent connections.

3. Did the study last long enough?

How long was the study's follow-up? Was it long enough to see whether the drug or other treatment can provide long-term benefits? How long do patients ordinarily survive with this disease? Were your patients followed long enough to really know the outcomes, good or bad?

Example: A new drug may put some cancer patients into remission—but it will take more time to see if the drug will lengthen survival. Many studies with these limitations still should be reported, but the limitations should be noted.

4. Are there other possible explanations for the findings? Any other reasons to question the conclusions?

Cause-and-effect?—Remember that association is not necessarily causation. A virus found in patients with a particular illness may not be the cause of that illness. A chemical found in the water supply may not be the cause of people's illnesses.

Always "view mathematical associations with a healthy degree of skepticism," cautions Dr. Michael Greenberg at Rutgers.

Yet, with care, researchers can build a case. A good experiment, controlling all variables, can sometimes prove cause and effect almost surely. A strong association coupled with lab or animal studies may be persuasive. In other cases, proof may be more elusive.

But when does a close association in an observational study (rather than a controlled experiment) indicate causation? There are several possible criteria that you can ask about while discussing the overall picture with a researcher:

- Is the association statistically strong (like the association between smoking and lung cancer)? And is the association consistent?
- Does the supposed cause precede the effect?
- Do high doses of a chemical (or something else) tend to cause more problems than lower doses? Heavy smokers are indeed at greater risk than moderate smokers, and moderate smokers at greater risk than light smokers. (With some things, there may a threshold effect, an effect only after some minimum dose.)
- Is the association consistent when different research methods are used?
- Does the association make biological sense? Does it agree with current biological and physiological knowledge? You can't follow this test out the window. Much biological fact is ill understood. Also, Harvard's Mosteller warns, "*Someone* nearly always will claim to see a [biological or physiological] association. But the people who know the most may not be willing to."[6]
- Did you look for other explanations—confounders, or confounding variables, that may be producing or helping produce the association? Sometimes we read that married people live longer than singles. Does marriage really increase life expectancy, or may medical or other problems make

some people less likely to marry and also die sooner? Maybe the Dutch thought storks brought babies because better-off families had more chimneys, more storks, and more babies. See "Eliminate Bias; Consider Alternate Explanations" in Chapter 3 for more examples.

Does a treatment really work?—Could the improvement in the patients' condition be due to something other than the new treatment they are receiving? Some questions to probe for other possible explanations:

Could the patients' improvements be changes that are occurring in the normal course of their disease? Some medical problems (multiple sclerosis, some forms of arthritis, etc.) have symptoms that tend to wax and wane; improvements may be due to the normal course of the illness rather than a new treatment being studied.

Could an old treatment that a patient received before the new one be responsible for a delayed improvement? Or, if a patient is receiving more than one treatment, which one is responsible for the improvement? Or might both be helping? When studying some alternative therapy, ask: Was the patient also receiving some conventional treatment that might have been responsible for the improvement?

If a treatment appears to work against one type of diabetes or pneumonia or heart problem or whatever, are you assuming that this will work against other types of that illness? What is the basis for that assumption? This is a particularly important area to probe in cancer treatments, where, for example, a treatment might help for one form of lung cancer, but not for other forms of lung cancer.

If all the patients in a study had an early or a mild form of an illness, you may need to ask the researcher: Why do you think your treatment will help patients with advanced or severe cases? But the reverse also can be true. Hospital populations and "worst cases" are not necessarily typical of patients in general. Be on guard against any improper generalization.

Even claims for medications that reduce symptoms of some minor ailments need to be questioned. Doctors often say, "Most things are better in the morning," and they're often right when it comes to minor aches and pains that tend to wax and wane. So: Is the patient feeling better because of the medications, or simply because of the tincture of time?

Careful design of the study and analysis of the data can help get at the answers for many of these questions and others as well.

Measuring what works—How did you know or decide when your patients were cured or improved? Were there explicit, objective outcome criteria? That is, were there firm measurements or test results rather than physicians' observations in interviews, physical examinations, or chart reviews—all techniques highly subject to great observer variation and inaccuracy?

In studies of improvement or relief from pain, which in some cases is a hard-to-quantify outcome, ask: Was there some systematic way of making an assessment? (When even a single patient says that she or he feels relief from pain, that's important for that patient. But only a careful study can make a judgment about whether a pain-relief technique is likely to help other patients as well.)

If two or more groups were compared for survival: Were they judged by the same disease definitions at the start, and the same measures of severity and outcome?

Looking for the bottom line—Did the intervention have the good results that were intended? Has there been an evaluation to see whether they were useful results?

Investigators often report that a drug or other measure has lowered cholesterol levels in the blood. Good. But were the investigators able to show that this particular method of cholesterol reduction cut the number of heart attacks? Or was the reduction of a supposed risk factor itself taken to mean the hoped-for outcome?

In such cases, the cholesterol reading (or other lab findings) is called a marker. If a new treatment lowers cholesterol levels in the blood, the researcher hopes that this means it also will reduce the risk of heart attacks. But that bottom-line answer can take time.

Questions the reporter can ask the researcher (and sometimes other experts): Is a particular lab test a reliable measure of final outcome? What's the evidence for that? What follow-up studies may be needed to get a conclusive answer?

Also watch out for unexpected effects and side effects of treatments. Investigators once reported that a new heart drug reduced the number of recurrent heart attacks, fatal and nonfatal. But total mortality from all causes was higher in the treated group than in a placebo group.

Another example of an area in which reporters need to keep their eyes on the bottom line: Public health officials may announce that, in a screening campaign, 200 people were found to have high blood pressure and were referred to their doctors. But how many then went to their doctors? How many of those received optimum treatment? Were their blood pressures reduced? (If they were, the evidence is strong that they should suffer fewer strokes.)

Did you really do any good? To whom do your results apply? Can they be generalized to a larger population? Are your patients like the average doctor's patients? Is there any basis in these findings for any patient to ask his or her doctor for a change in treatment? Clinic populations, hospital populations, and the "worst cases" are not necessarily typical of patients in general, and improper generalization is unfortunately common in the medical literature.

Finding what breakdowns can reveal—Some questions that you can ask researchers about various types of studies:

Did you do a stratified analysis—a breakdown of the data by strata such as gender, race, socio-economic status, geographical area, occupation?

Men commonly have more cirrhosis of the liver than women because they drink more. They also have more heart disease, possibly because they've smoked longer, possibly because some hormones protect women.

A treatment may work better for women than for men, or vice versa.

Stratified analyses will bring out such differences.

5. Do the conclusions fit other evidence?

Are your results consistent with other experimental findings and knowledge in the field? If not, why? Have your results been repeated or confirmed or supported by other studies?

Virtually no single study proves anything. Consistency of results among human trials, animal experiments, and laboratory tests is a good start. Two or more studies in humans can build even more confidence.

One scientist warns, however, "You have to be wary about a grab bag of studies with different populations and different circumstances." To this Mosteller adds, "Yes, be wary, but consistency across such differences cheers me up."

Meta-analysis is the statistical analysis of several low-power research studies to integrate the results. In effect, it adds several studies together to try to come up with stronger conclusions. The trick is to make sure that the researcher adds only apples to apples. Dr. John Bailar tells us that, despite possible pitfalls, "meta-analysis of several low-power reports *may* come to stronger conclusions than any one of them alone" [italics ours].[7]

6. Do I have the full picture? What about side effects, cost issues, and ethical concerns?

Are there important side effects from a new drug (or other new treatment) being studied? Any other problems? Do the potential benefits outweigh these problems?

If it's a weight-loss or other type of diet, is it reasonable to expect that people will follow your diet?

Have any ethical problems arisen during the research? Do you see any ethical problems ahead?

What would the new treatment (or lab test or whatever) cost? Do the potential benefits outweigh the costs?

Example of a costs-benefits debate: In the summer of 1999, the U.S. Food and Drug Administration approved a new inhaled drug to treat influenza, overruling a panel of advisers who had concluded that the new drug was only marginally effective. But in Great Britain—the home base of the drug's maker, Glaxo Wellcome PLC—the government-run National Health Service ordered physicians not to prescribe the drug, after an advisory group there concluded that the costs "would be disproportionate to the benefits obtained by influenza sufferers."[8]

7. Have the findings been checked by other experts?

Ask the researcher: Who disagrees with you? And why?

Ask others in the same field: How do other informed people regard this report—and these investigators? Are they speaking in their own area of expertise, or have they shown real mastery if they have ventured outside it? Have their past results generally held up? And what are some good questions I can ask them? True, a lot of brilliant and original work has been pooh-poohed for a time by others. Still, scientists survive only by eventually convincing their colleagues.

Has there been a review of the data and conclusions by any disinterested parties?

Medicine and health—Have the study and its findings been examined by peer-review referees who were sent the article by a journal editor? Has the work been published or accepted by a reputable journal? If not, why not?

Medical meetings also are an important source of news. But research papers presented at meetings normally have not been reviewed with the rigor used by good medical journals to select the papers they publish. So reporters may need to ask more questions or, if they attend the meeting, listen to what other experts at the session say.

Some free-circulation journals and medical magazines, supported totally by advertising, print summary articles rather than original research reports. These articles normally are not as rigorously screened as those published in the traditional journals. They may make news too, but the limits on their peer-review process should be kept in mind.

Other fields—Peer-reviewed journal articles and meetings also are important sources of news in other fields ranging from economics to crime prevention.

But many people outside academia do studies in various nonhealth fields, and these studies may never be sent to journals or be presented at major meetings. Many good economics reports and environmental studies fit into this category.

It's still fair to ask these researchers whether their conclusions have been checked by independent experts. The answers may help you determine how deeply you want to probe with other questions.

Top journals—In science as a whole, including biology and other basic medical sciences, *Science* and the British *Nature* are indispensable.

In general medicine and clinical science at the physician's level, the most useful journals include (but aren't limited to) the *New England Journal of Medicine,* the *Journal of the American Medical Association,* and the British *Lancet.*

In epidemiology, a good source, among others, is the *American Journal of Epidemiology.* Some important epidemiological studies are reported in the *New England Journal of Medicine* and other clinically oriented journals.

There are many equally good medical specialty journals, as well as mediocre ones. Ask people in any field: What are the most reliable journals, those where you would want your work published?

Warning label—Peer review can not provide a guarantee. Even the best of journals can print clinkers sometimes.

"Scientific journals are records of work, not of revealed truth," says the *New England Journal of Medicine*'s Dr. Arnold Relman.[9]

8. What now?

What do you think should happen now?

If it's a basic research finding, ask: How could your finding eventually be put to use to help people?

If it's a new treatment that's only been studied in the lab, ask: What steps must be taken to get this new treatment tried in patients?

If already tried in some patients, ask: What steps remain before this treatment can be approved for widespread use?

In all these cases, ask: How long should this take? What is the potential? What could go wrong? Are other researchers working on different approaches that could compete with your approach? How much weight should your work be given? Is it really firm? And how important?

The Bottom Line

Mostly just good-sense questions? Of course. Some of the most important questions of all for a reporter to ponder are these: What do I think? Do the conclusions make sense to me? Do the data really justify the conclusions? If this person has extrapolated beyond the evidence, has he or she explained why and made sense?*

Does the investigator frankly document or discuss the possible biases and flaws in the study? It's a big plus for the researcher who does. Does the investigator admit that the conclusion may be tentative or equivocal? Dr. Robert Boruch at Northwestern University says, "It requires audacity and some courage to say, 'I don't know.'"[10]

Do the authors use qualifying phrases? If such phrases are important, reporters should share them with their readers or viewers.

Read the journal article yourself, if there is one. Ask the researcher for a copy. Or check the Internet where some journals' articles are now available. Or phone the journal. Or look for it at a medical library, which can be found at any medical college and many hospitals. Too many news releases tout articles that read far more conservatively than the PR version.

"What proportion of papers will satisfy [all] the requirements for scientific proof and clinical applicability?" Sackett writes. "Not very many. . . . After all, there are only a handful of ways to do a study properly but a thousand ways to do it wrong."[11]

Despite impeccable design, some studies yield answers that turn out to be wrong. Some fail for lack of understanding of physiology and disease. Even the soundest studies may provoke controversy. In particular, some "may meet considerable resistance when they discredit the only treatment currently available," Sackett says.

Reporters need to tread a narrow path between believing everything and believing nothing. Also—we are reporters—some of the controversies make good stories.

Also keep in mind:

"Hindsight bias"—As with much of life, it's easier to see some problems in retrospect. After a study is completed, reporters may see how a study could have been better designed to find more answers.

Journalists should ask themselves: Should the researcher have been able to foresee the problem at the start of the study? Or did the researcher simply overlook something that any researcher might have overlooked?

The answers should determine how the journalist reports the study's limitations. And sometimes this should be done gently, pointing out the everyday comparison with seeing things in hindsight.

Basic research—Some genetic, cell-function, and other research is at such a basic level that researchers say they don't know how their findings could be put to use. Reporters should realize that such findings can be important building blocks for later scientific advances. Scientists should realize that unless someone can envision future uses, important basic findings may or may not be news.

Checklist—See "Checklists for Studies and Polls" in the Appendix for a quick-reference list of this chapter's eight areas to consider in assessing a study.

Tests and Testing: Measuring What Works

6

Testing is often the only way to answer our questions, but it doesn't produce unassailable, universal truths that should be carved on stone tablets. Instead, testing produces statistics, which must be interpreted.

—Robert Hooke

Who knows when thou mayest be tested?

—Ronald Arthur Hopwood

 *&* *&* *&*

Questions about new drugs, vaccines and medical tests can pop up in all sorts of ways. A couple of examples:

• A body scanning method called spiral CT scanning has demonstrated its ability to find lung cancer when the tumor is as small in diameter as a soda straw. Chest X-rays typically don't show this type of tumor until they are the size of a quarter, almost always too late to help. But will this new scanning technique save lives? Even though it can find lung cancer earlier than has been possible before, will it be early enough—before this type of cancer spreads out of control?[1]

Simply because a new test works doesn't guarantee that it will be medically useful. Only careful testing and analysis of the resulting numbers can do that.

• A new vaccine against the rota-virus—which is a major cause of severe, sometimes life-threatening diarrhea in infants—had to be taken off the market in late 1999. More than 100 babies unexpectedly had developed serious bowel obstructions after receiving the vaccine. Two had died.[2]

After initial approval of any new drug and vaccine, more and more patients are likely to use it. This increases the chances that rare, but serious, side effects will begin to show up.

Patients' Tests

False Negatives and Positives

A good test should detect both health and disease, and do so with high accuracy. The measures of the value of a clinical test, one used for medical diagnosis, are sensitivity and specificity, or simply the ability to avoid false negatives and false positives.

Sensitivity is how well a test identifies a disease or condition in those who have it. It is how well the test avoids false negatives, or missed cases.

Example: If 100 people with an illness are tested and 90 test positive, the test's sensitivity is 90 percent.

Specificity is how well a test identifies those who do *not* have the disease or condition. It is how well the test avoids false positives, or mistaken identifications.

Example: If 100 healthy people are tested and 90 test negative, the test's specificity is 90 percent.

In a nutshell: Sensitivity tells us about disease present. Specificity tells us about disease absent.

If the terms were used with home burglar alarms, sensitivity would reflect how well the system will detect an actual burglar. Specificity would reflect how prone the system is to false alarms.

Almost every test produces some false positives and some false negatives, and the two qualities are inversely related. The more sensitive you make a test to try to find every case, the less specific it will be and the more false positives you will get. The more specific you make it to try to avoid false labeling, the less sensitive it will be and the more false negatives you will get.

Testing the Tests

The main questions that a reporter needs to ask the person who unveils a new test for AIDS or cancer or diabetes are, How many false negatives and false positives do you get? How do you know this? Have you done an adequate trial?

A new test should be tried and assessed by blinded observers in subjects chosen, by some definitive diagnosis, as patients who have the condition being sought. (This diagnosis may be by surgery, biopsy, long-term follow-up, or some other precise method.)

The new test should be tried as well in healthy people, and often it should also be tried in some people who have a condition frequently confused with the one being studied.

How well should a test do in avoiding false negatives and false positives? That may depend on its goal.

If the main aim is not to miss some serious condition, the test may shoot for high sensitivity to pick up every possible case, and accept the false negatives.

If the main concern is avoiding false positives in a disease doctors can't do much about anyway, or if the treatment itself carries significant danger, one may opt for more specificity.

Doubt was expressed about some tests for strep throat, because in 25 reports their sensitivity ranged from a reasonably acceptable 93 percent to an unacceptably low 65 percent. In short, there were too many false negatives for this illness. (Nevertheless, researchers sometimes have to accept poor sensitivity in a test for a particular disease, if it's the best they can do. A poor test may be better than no test.)

A study group evaluated one firm's home pregnancy-testing kits whose maker claimed they detected pregnancy 95 to 98 percent of the time. Testing them in 144 pregnant women, the study group found them only 75.6 percent sensitive—one false negative in every four tests.[3]

Other potential questions about the testing of tests:

• Is this the right test for this particular condition? Epidemiologist Gary Friedman offered this example: Measuring a heart rate by putting your fingers on someone's wrist (taking a radial pulse) would lack validity for some patients with certain disturbances in heart rhythm, because some of their heartbeats produce too weak a pulse to be felt at the wrist.[4]

• How reliable, or reproducible, is the test? Does a series of observations produce the same or nearly the same result? If the results of a test typically vary, it must be repeated, perhaps several times, to get a mean and a more reliable result.

But you should recognize that some results may vary through no fault of the test. For example, your blood pressure may be different when you are relaxed and when you are tense.

All tests are subject to error. Results can be affected by diet, drugs, exposure of a blood sample to light, a malfunctioning instrument, or a cockeyed observer.

There are some test results that don't have numbers. These include such things as listening for heart murmurs and studying the wavy lines on an electrocardiogram for telltale clues about the heart. While trained people do these tests well, there can be more room for subjective judgments and differing opinions.

The lesson, if you're a patient or are writing about patients: Be cautious about letting yourself (or anyone else) be sentenced to a dire diagnosis on the basis of any one test. Still, one bone-marrow examination may indicate leukemia; one X-ray may clearly show a fracture.

- What's normal? There is also a potential trap in the word "normal." Some testers use it to mean average or statistically typical. Others use it to mean healthy or desirable or free of disease. "Within the normal range," a phrase often used, can mean little unless explained.

Example: Someone tells you that your serum cholesterol—the amount of cholesterol in your blood—is 210 (milligrams per deciliter) and that's not much above average for adult Americans. But it is too high to be optimal in the view of physicians who think it's associated with an elevated risk of atherosclerosis, or clogged arteries.

Similarly "abnormal" may just mean that a particular laboratory finds you're in the top or bottom 5 or 10 percent of test results at that lab or some group of labs. Thus "abnormal" might or might not mean anything clinically, anything affecting your health.

Ask: Does "normal" mean average, or does it mean okay? Does "abnormal" mean atypical or unhealthy?

• Can any test find the answer? Few tests, however negative the result, are sure enough to give us a "clean bill of health."

Example: In January 1987 a usually excellent radio news program said tests on President Reagan had ruled out any spread of his earlier cancer. But cancer's spread is often undetectable and therefore unmeasurable, though it may later manifest itself. Such tests could only show that no spread of cancer had been found. In assessing health or disease, a good physician considers the results of a combination of several tests, as well as physical signs, symptoms, your behavior, and your history.

Screening Tests

In addition to clinical tests to investigate some complaint, there are screening tests of normal persons, designed to pick out those who might have some condition but need further examination to confirm it.

Examples: routine Pap smears, mammograms, the tuberculin test to find those exposed to the TB bacillus, multiphasic testing for many conditions.

Keep in mind:

• A screening test should not be so rough that it exposes hundreds or thousands of actually healthy people to worry and expense, to possibly harmful further testing by chemical or invasive means, or to possibly harmful surgery or other treatment.

• Studies that try to assess screening tests can be deceiving. People who take better care of themselves—or, perversely, those most likely to have the disease—may self-select themselves as test subjects.

• Many authorities think society should forgo screening programs unless a test of demonstrated value attacks an important health problem that doctors can do something about at a cost within reason.

Drugs and Drug Trials

Many authorities recommend mistrusting any doctor who says, "Don't worry. I've been using this drug for years, and I've never seen these adverse reactions you read about." For starters, this physician may not be seeing the types of patients most vulnerable (by age, race, etc.) to side effects. But even more important, no single doctor can be seeing enough patients to make sweeping claims about safety.

By one calculation, "the individual physician is in a functional sense 'blind' to treatment-related risk" that occurs any less commonly than once in about 200 patients.[5] Drugs have been withdrawn or forced into restricted use because of adverse reactions in the range of 1 in 1,000 to 1 in 30,000.

Are such drug withdrawals good or bad for society and for patients? The Food and Drug Administration, which judges drugs, is alternately attacked as the protector of venal drug companies foisting harmful drugs on the public, and as the citadel of needless regulation that denies good drugs to patients and profits to businesses.

The best course is not always easy to decide. If you're the 1 patient in 30,000 who is dead, you're very dead. But would withdrawing the drug cause many more deaths in people who might have been saved by it?

By and large, all that was said in the last chapter on questions reporters can ask applies to drugs and medications. When a scientist or a company comes forth with a new drug, or with a new use for an old one, ask: How do you know it works? What is your evidence?

Warning: You aren't likely to find many of the answers in most of the elaborate press kits that accompany the commercial release of many drugs.

Drug trials, by FDA rules, are conducted in *phases*—which are hurdles that must be leaped before a drug can win FDA approval.

In a Phase I trial a new drug is tested in humans for the first time. It has already been studied first *in vitro* ("in glass"), in test tubes (or petri dishes or beakers or flasks), then *in vivo* ("in something living"), in animals. In Phase I, the investigator tests for human toxicity and for other physiological responses, seeking a dosage range and schedule of acceptable toxicity. Typically 20 to 80 people (who may be healthy) get the drug in this phase. The doses studied are at first small, then gradually larger.

In Phase II the drug is tried in more patients (100 to 300) to establish dosages that might do some good. Again, there may be studies of various doses, schedules, and safety margins. Some Phase II studies are, like those in Phase I, open studies, with doctors and patients knowing that a new compound is being tested. Other Phase II studies are randomized and blinded.

Phase III means a full-scale clinical trial or trials to pit the drug against other treatments or no treatment. This is the last step. Before winning FDA approval, it may take years and typically involves 1,000 to 3,000 patients.

Ideally Phase III trials should be fully randomized, blinded studies comparing comparable groups of patients. For reasons of necessity or expense, they are sometimes less perfect. They are sometimes crossover studies (the same patients getting one treatment, then another), and sometimes trials comparing the patients with past medical records (historical controls).

Keep in mind that there are differences in physiological response from patient to patient. There are some spontaneous recoveries, along with the placebo effect in which some patients respond to anything they are given. All these things make drug testing at its best something less than a gold-plated assurance that a drug is now "safe" (or really, safe enough to be used) and effective.

But the greatest problem of all is that 1,000 or 3,000 patients are few compared with the many more thousands or even millions who may have to get a drug before all its effects and their frequencies become known. The real safety test of a drug is its use by doctors in general, on patients in general.

It is in this "big but poorly controlled experiment," by one description, that the life-threatening events often turn up. If a drug produces an unwarranted reaction in, say, 1 out of every 25,000 patients, the drug would have to be taken by a quarter-million people to produce 10 such reactions.

Case history: The antibiotic chloramphenicol (Chloromycetin) was approved and given to some 5 million people before the FDA decided that it caused serious blood disorders and death in 1 in perhaps 24,000 to 40,000 patients. The FDA then limited the drug's approved indications to a small number of infections, most commonly typhoid fever, and, when no other drug works, some eye, ear, and skin disorders. Some doctors who said they had never seen an adverse reaction continued using the drug more indiscriminately for years, and reports of deaths kept piling up.

A physician may legally use any licensed drug for any purpose, not just the use approved by the FDA. This is called *off-label* use. The doctor does so at the risk of a malpractice suit if the use is unreasonable, but there often is a rational basis for doing so.

In addition, hundreds of doctors, typically in academic medical centers, are using some unlicensed, experimental drugs on patients under FDA investigational permits.

You can read about licensed prescription drugs, including their noncapitalized generic or scientific names, their capitalized trade names, and their possible side effects and approved uses, in the *Physicians' Desk Reference,* or *PDR*—and about many nonprescription drugs in the *PDR for Non-Prescription Drugs.* But prescription drugs are described in the language approved by the FDA as the labeling or package insert usually seen by pharmacists, not by patients.

Reading about all the possible side effects of a drug can be frightening—at times, perhaps unnecessarily so. Dr. Gary Friedman notes that "companies tend to include every possible side effect that has been reported, probably to protect themselves."[6] Just the same, a reporter writing about a drug should read the full text.

For more about drug trials, see clinicaltrials.gov, a federal National Institutes of Health web site.

Animals as Stand-Ins for Us

Animals are the most common research subjects of all. Mice and rats are tested by the millions, other animals by the hundreds or thousands.

Animals are often much like people in their reactions, and often very different. The challenge to scientists is to pick the right animal model for the subject—the human disease or risk or physiological change—that is being studied. Armadillos are reasonable models for the study of leprosy, cats for deafness, mice for cancer and epilepsy, rats for diabetes and aging, pigs for heart disease, and dogs for many conditions.

But no animal is a completely satisfactory model for any human disease. Cortisone causes cleft palate in mice but not in humans. A dose of morphine that can kill a human merely anesthetizes a dog. Arsenic doesn't induce cancer in animals but does in man.

It's often said that "mice are not men." But in some ways, animals are superior to human beings as research subjects. No experimenter can control all human variables, but a scientist can select an inbred strain of mice with common genetics to make sure that this variability isn't confusing the experiment. One more *example:* It's easy to control diet in animals, and often tough in humans.

When it comes to determining whether a substance is cancer-causing or has other toxic worries, dosages often must be far higher in animals than in typical human exposures. It takes both large dosages and large numbers of subjects to get an answer in mice, which live only a few years, in a reasonable time at an affordable cost.

Animal studies are not without possible biases. Animals, like people, vary from day to day in their physiology and behavior. The position of a cage in a room may affect response; careful researchers rotate cages to avoid this *cage effect.* Animals sometimes have undetected infections.

The most difficult problem is the problem of extrapolating from animals to man. Animals can nonetheless alert us to potential uses for drugs and potential problems of chemicals and other agents. There are many classic animal experiments. In 1945 Howard Florey and Ernst Chain infected mice with streptococci, then injected some of them with the new experimental drug penicillin. All of the untreated mice were dead by the next day; all the treated mice lived.

In extrapolating from animals to man, said a 1984 scientific panel, "the characterization of human risk always requires interdisciplinary evaluation of the entire array of data"—laboratory, animal, and human—"on a case by case basis."[7]

In short, it requires human judgment. And the
reporter asking a scientist about an animal experiment
should ask much the same questions one would ask about
a human experiment.

Were there controls? Were there possible biases?
What were the numbers? Is this a good animal species for
this test? Do you think you can extrapolate? What is the
biological and medical significance for humans?

Vital Statistics: Measuring Life and Health

7

If I had known I was going to live this long, I would have taken better care of myself.

—Casey Stengel, on turning 80

I said to a patient who was an undertaker, "I'm curious. How did you happen to pick me as your physician?" He replied: "Nothing to it. I checked the records and found you wrote the fewest death certificates."

—Dr. Philip R. Alper in *Medical Economics*

"Jes' don't die, I guess."

—A Southern centenarian when asked by a TV reporter, "What should we do to live a long time?"

We can brag about some of our nation's vital statistics. Our nation's death rate is at a record low, and life expectancy is at an all-time high.

Other vital statistics show us where we can improve. The infant mortality rate varies greatly across the country. It ranges from 4.3 infant deaths for every 1,000 live births in New Hampshire, to 10.6 in Mississippi, at this writing. And in Sweden it's only 3.6.[1]

Still other vital statistics may surprise us. The death rate in New York City during the first week of the year 2000 was up 50 percent over the comparable week of 1999. Neither influenza nor any other disease outbreak could explain it.

Experts concluded that many terminally ill people pushed themselves to live longer to see the new millennium arrive—much as, other experts believe, some other people live longer to enjoy a major event like a family wedding.[2]

Vital statistics track the numbers and trends of births, deaths, diseases, and other life events, such as marriages and divorces. They allow us to measure the progress—or lack of it—that our nation, our states, and our cities are making against all sorts of diseases. And they often chronicle the cost and other burdens of illnesses as well.

There are breakdowns, breakdowns, and breakdowns of the figures. We can look at national, state, local, and other data. Vital statistics break down cancer and other diseases by gender, age groups, and in many other ways.

As reporters, we can use these figures to write articles about where we stand, where trends appear to be taking us, and to compare our community's experience with the nation's.

The Key Role of Rates in Vital Statistics

John Graunt, a 17th century Englishman who was a pioneer in vital statistics, calculated London's three leading causes of deaths in 1632. He called them "chrisomes and infants" (which meant infant deaths, since chrisomes were used as burial robes for babies); "consumption" (tuberculosis and probably cancer and other wasting diseases); and "fever."

(In this day of antibiotics and other treatments that have lengthened the average life expectancy, the three leading causes of death in the United States are, in order, heart disease, cancer, and strokes.)

Graunt also developed rates and proportions as ways to describe what he saw, and pointed out how such data might be used to spot problems. "There is much pleasure," he wrote, "in deducing so many abstruse, and unexpected inferences."[3]

Not until the mid–19th century did registration of births and causes of death become at all regular in both the United States and Britain, but Graunt's rates remain central to measuring nature's continuing experiment that is life.

A rate, to a statistician, is a specific kind of proportion. A percentage is a proportion too. But a rate always expresses its numerator and its stated or implied denominator or baseline, as "so many per so many" per unit of time. A rate is a way of describing a group. It answers the question: Compared with whom? Or compared with what?

Key Rates of Death and Disease

The two most commonly used medical rates—incidence and prevalence—are often confused, even in the medical literature.

An incidence rate is the number of persons who get a disease, divided by the total number at risk (or total given population), per unit of time.

Example: The incidence rate of disease A is three percent a year in the United States. That is, in any given year, about three percent of all Americans develop this illness.

Incidence measures only new cases or, strictly, new cases that are diagnosed. Often the true incidence can only be estimated.

A prevalence rate of a disease is the total rate, of both new cases and old cases, in a given population at a given time. It is the total number of persons affected at that time divided by the total population.

If incidence is like an entering class, prevalence is the whole school.

Example: The prevalence rate of condition A in the screening exam at the plant was one percent.

(The word "rate" is often assumed in many incidence and prevalence rates.)

Case rate is a term sometimes used to mean a disease's prevalence rate, with *new case rate* referring to the incidence. But be careful—all these terms are often used loosely or carelessly.

Other rates for deaths and illness:

A mortality rate is the incidence of *deaths* per unit of time in a community, nation, or group.

A morbidity rate is the equivalent rate of a *particular disease* or, sometimes, all illness.

Years of potential life lost (YPLL) is a measure of premature mortality. It ranks causes of deaths by measuring the number of years of life lost, rather than number of lives lost.

For YPLL, experts calculate the years lost from a relatively normal life expectancy of 75 years. For example, a person who dies of heart disease at age 73 counts as only a few years of life lost. A 13-year-old girl who dies in a traffic accident counts as more than 60 years of life lost.

Accidents are the nation's number five cause of death while calculated in the traditional each-death-counts-as-one way. But accidents rise to number three in YPLL calculations (still behind heart disease and cancer), because many accidental deaths occur at relatively young ages.

YPLL is a good way of looking at prevention potential, but it best supplements rather than replaces the regular mortality rate.

Crude Rates versus Rates That Compare

We said that rates answer the question: Compared with what? There are several basic ways of describing populations or groups so they can be compared.

A crude rate, whether an incidence, mortality, or prevalence rate, simply tells you the number of cases or whatever in a population. It is important to know, but it's no help if you want to know where the disease is concentrated.

A group-specific rate can more tellingly state the number of cases in some subgroup, that is, what proportion of what group is affected.

An age-specific rate, or an age- and gender-specific rate, is often given in 5- or 10-year groupings.

A case-fatality rate is the number of persons dying of a disease divided by the total number who have it. This may be stated per unit of time, or simply as the proportion who eventually die of the condition.

The maternal mortality rate is the number of maternal deaths attributed to childbirth in a year, divided by total live births.

An attack rate is the cumulative count of new cases (in relation to a total population, without specifying a unit of time). But it is commonly used in connection with a specific epidemic or—a term with less emotional charge—outbreak of a disease.

When you need to compare two groups and they differ in some important way—say, in age—you need an *adjusted* or *standardized rate.*

An age-adjusted rate uses some method to calculate what would happen if the two groups were comparable in age distribution. One method of arriving at an age-adjusted rate is to choose some standard population—the

U.S. population in a particular year, for example—and
calculate the number of cases that would occur if the
population you are looking at had the same distribution.

Example: The age-adjusted rate for Florida would tell
you what Florida's rate would be if that state wasn't a
retirement mecca but had a more normal distribution of
younger people.

True, you are now dealing with a contrived rate that
does not truly describe the population. For that you may
need a crude rate. Yet for many purposes an adjusted rate
gives you a clearer picture.

One statistician says, "I think group-specific rates give
you the clearest picture of a disease. But say you want to
compare two cities. If you just want to know the prevalence of a disease in the two, you should know the crude
rates—after all, they tell you how big a problem each city
has. But if you want to know why the two cities differ, you
must adjust, ideally, by age, gender, race, income, and
often occupation. And you'll know even more if you also
compare the group-specific rates in the two."

If you did not age-adjust U.S. cancer rates when comparing them from decade to decade, you would not be
taking into account that people have been living long
enough to get cancer instead of dying from other diseases.

An adjusted rate gives you what statisticians call an
expected rate compared with the actual observed rate.

Friedman points out that you might want to compare the lung cancer rate in a group of smokers with that
in some nonsmokers of various ages. You want to compare the results of smoking, not age, so you age-adjust
the nonsmokers' lung cancer rate to the rate you'd
expect if they were the same age as the smokers. You can
now more accurately see the effect of cigarettes on the
smokers.[4]

You'll sometimes see a reference to the *magnitude* of
a difference between two groups. That's just its size. Say

one group has 100 more cases of a disease than another, or one has a 50 percent greater rate. Those figures are the magnitudes of the difference.

Putting Numbers on Risks

A difference between two incidence or prevalence rates can be called an *excess rate* or *excess risk*—and an attributable risk if there is a difference in some variable, like cigarette smoking, strongly believed to cause the difference. Investigators like to say the guilty variable has a "causal role." But that's a phrase you may want to avoid in print since a typo (or a quick reading) too often changes it to a "casual" role.

You can usefully compare two rates by calculating the ratio of one to the other—that is, dividing one by the other. This gives you the *relative risk,* or *risk ratio.*

Example: If disease A occurs in 50 cases per 100,000 in group X and in 200 per 100,000 in group Y, group Y's risk is four times greater than group X's. This is commonly expressed as a relative risk of 4.

You'll often see a lower number for a relative risk, such as 1.3 or 1.5—that is, a 30 or 50 percent increased chance of disease, death, exposure, or whatever. A reported relative risk that small may or may not signal a problem, given the limited reliability of observation and other possible variables. Any risk ratio of less than 2.0 is a signal for a reporter to ask more questions.

Example of a particularly strong risk ratio: In an American Cancer Society smoking study, the lung cancer mortality rate in nonsmokers aged 55 to 69 was 19 per 100,000 per year; the risk in smokers was 188 per 100,000. Since 188 divided by 19 equals 9.89, the smokers were about 9.9 times more likely to die from lung cancer—their relative risk was 9.9.[5]

Example of a relatively small risk ratio: A disease has a background rate (normal occurrence) of 50 cases per 100,000 people. A study finds 65 cases per 100,000 workers who are occupationally exposed to a certain chemical. This is an increased risk of 30 percent, for a relative risk of 1.3. Other evidence may be needed to show that the chemical is the culprit for this relatively small increase.

To introduce another term: The greater the odds of an association, the greater the *strength* of the association.

As important as it can be, a risk-ratio figure standing alone doesn't give the full picture. It doesn't tell how many people are at the increased risk—for example, how many people smoke.

And in total lives affected, a large risk ratio for a rare condition may not be as important as a smaller risk ratio for a common illness such as breast cancer.

Two Cautions

States are ranked, from best to worst, in everything from infant mortality rates to divorce rates. But often there are only minor differences between some of the states on these lists. The 27th-ranked state may be doing almost as well as the 17th-ranked state. These minor differences also can result in large year-to-year changes in your state's position on a list.

The lesson: It's often helpful to report these rankings. It's more helpful, to your readers or viewers, when you point out that your state is close to several other states.

Percentage increases sometimes can be misleading too. A disease outbreak may start with, say, three reported cases. By the time there are 33 cases, there will have been a 1,000 percent increase! By contrast, when 95 percent of a state's youngsters have been immunized against a particular disease, it's impossible to have a large percentage increase.

The lesson: When you start with a small base, any significant gain is likely to be large in percentage terms. Use caution so that you don't hype the figures.

Cancer Statistics

Cancer Rates and Cancer "Cures"

What's a cure? Normally it means no more evidence of disease, no recurrence, and a normal life expectancy that would be expected without the disease in question. But for cancer, some doctors and others sometimes talk of 5-year and occasionally 10-year "cure rates." With many types of cancer, most patients, but not all, who survive five years will have no recurrence.

The 10-year rate is sometimes cited too. And it should be, to be honest, for breast cancer and prostate cancer— just two examples of cancers with many deaths after 5 or even 10 years later.

Cancer statistics normally use *relative survival rates,* which measure the chance of survival from cancer. More about that term in a moment.

Here are the latest figures from the federal National Cancer Institute at this writing in 2000:[6]

The 5-year relative survival rate for U.S. patients with cancer—at all sites in the body combined—is now 59 percent. The comparable 10-year relative survival rate is 48 percent.

The 5-year relative survival rate for U.S. women with breast cancer is now 85 percent. The comparable 10-year rate is 71 percent, and the 15-year rate is even lower; such is breast cancer's oft-long-delayed toll.

In short, the fact that not all cancer patients will survive means no one can truly tell until years later who are cured and who are not. Strictly speaking, a cure should mean only that the patient very certainly does not have the disease anymore. Thus, it is more accurate to report 5-year and 10-year "relative survival rates," rather than calling them "cure rates."

A bit more about cancer survival rates:

Absolute survival (also called *observed survival)* is simply the actual proportion of patients still alive after X years, considering deaths from all causes, cancer or otherwise.

Relative survival, the preferred figure, is calculated by adjusting the observed survival to take into account the normal life expectancy of a similar population. In effect, you gauge the effect of cancer alone by removing the effect of all other causes of death—heart attack, auto accidents, shootings, or whatever.

Too many news stories skip mentioning that they are dealing with relative survival. The story may say "59 percent of cancer patients survive." To be honest, we should explain relative survival and use terms like "survive from cancer" or "survive the effects of cancer." More than half of all Americans who get cancer are already 65 and older, so it's not surprising that many die of other causes.

An important explanation of "cancer sites" terms:

- "All sites" means cancer occurring anywhere in the body. It means all types of cancer with one major exception: Most forms of skin cancers, those that are relatively easy to cure, are not counted in all-sites incidence and survival rates. Melanoma is the only skin cancer included in these rates. (But overall cancer mortality rates include all cancer deaths.)
- A cancer site (lung cancer, breast cancer, whatever) refers to where the cancer started. Colon cancer, for example, may spread to the liver, but it's still

classified as colon cancer because that's where it started in the body.

Are We Gaining on Cancer?

Are new cancer cases increasing or decreasing? Are the chances of surviving increasing? The answers are generally encouraging. But like so much in medicine, there are caveats. The following are the latest cancer figures for the United States, for all races combined, at this writing in 2000:

New cases—After increasing during the period from 1973 to 1990, the all-sites cancer incidence rate has begun to edge downward slightly.

The cancer incidence rate measures the probability of getting cancer by calculating the number of *newly diagnosed cases* per 100,000 Americans per year.

There's a mixed picture when you break down the incidence rate. For example, a big drop in cigarette smoking since the mid-1960s has pushed down the lung cancer incidence rate. But the breast cancer incidence rate has shown little change. And the incidence rates for non-Hodgkin's lymphoma and melanoma skin cancer have risen.

A warning from the National Cancer Institute and the American Cancer Society: Unless recent increases in adolescent smoking can be reversed, declining lung cancer incidence rates are likely to start increasing again. Lung cancer, with a low survival rate, already is the nation's leading cause of cancer deaths.[7]

Survival rate trends—For all sites in the body combined, the latest available five-year relative survival rate, 59 percent, is up from 50 percent in the mid-1970s.

The increasing push for early detection of breast, prostate, and some other types of cancer is helping. Early detection can find these types of cancers at stages where they are more likely to be treated successfully.

But early detection also can cause a statistical quirk that's called *lead-time bias*. By finding cancer earlier, it starts the "survival-rate clock" running earlier. That can make the apparent length of survival seem longer, when it may not actually be so. *Example:* Say a cancer is detected two years earlier than it otherwise would have been found. For that reason alone, the patient would be expected to survive two years longer from the time of the diagnosis.

Death rate trends—Because of this *lead-time bias,* many experts believe the best way of looking at overall progress against cancer is the death rate.

The nation's overall, age-adjusted cancer death rate fell slightly in the 1990s. The death rate is the number of cancer deaths per 100,000 Americans.

This overall figure doesn't tell you about a particular type of cancer or what has been happening in white males, white females, black males, black females, or other groups. But all these figures, and many more, are available. Here are some examples:

By race—The 59 percent relative survival rate for all races breaks down to 61 percent for whites but only 48 percent for blacks. (Smoking patterns, diet, genetics, some barriers to medical care, and other factors may play roles in racial differences for various cancer statistics.)[8]

By cancer sites—Cancer is many different diseases with one thing in common: uncontrolled growth and spread of abnormal cells. Statistics differ markedly from one type of cancer to another. The five-year relative survival rate for liver cancer is 5 percent; for lung cancer, 14 percent; for thyroid cancer, 95 percent.

By factors that affect individual patients—Survival rates and other statistics also are available for various subtypes of cancer—for example, different types of lung cancer. And breakdown statistics are available for the *staging* of the cancer—whether it has started to spread, or how far it has spread. These breakdowns can be particularly important for people who have cancer, and for the doctors and nurses who treat them. And it can be important if you are writing about a public figure or someone else who has cancer.

Our advice to reporters: Look at all three major types of cancer statistics—incidence, survival, and mortality. And talk with more than one expert. Ask how the three ways of reducing the cancer toll—prevention, early detection, and treatment—may apply to a particular type of cancer or a specific situation.

And keep in mind how many people might be helped. Even a limited gain that is achieved against a common type of cancer (whether from prevention, early detection, or treatment) could save many more lives than a "cure" for a rare form of cancer.

"Lifetime Risk" and "Cancer Clusters"

Two types of cancer figures deserve special cautions.

The "one-in-nine" controversy—You may read or hear that a "woman has a one in nine risk of developing breast cancer in her lifetime." Some doctors, reporters, and others use such *lifetime risk* numbers to encourage women to have early-detection mammograms—a noble goal. But lifetime risk estimates can be misleading unless accompanied by caveats, which too often are missing.

In "Putting the Risk of Breast Cancer in Perspective" in the *New England Journal of Medicine* and in a follow-up letter to the editors of that journal, doctors noted: Breast cancer lifetime estimates really mean that an *average* woman has a statistical one-in-nine risk of developing breast cancer *at some point* over the course of her *entire* lifetime. The risk in any single year of life—or even decade of life—is much lower. The older the woman, the greater that risk.[9]

All such estimates are necessarily based on current trends, which could change over time. And some women have higher, some lower, risks than the average, based on family history of breast cancer and other factors.[10] The doctors urged the news media to avoid scary generalizations. They also might remind women that heart disease is the number one killer of women.

The American Cancer Society now uses age-group breakdowns that can be helpful. The society, in its "Cancer Facts and Figures 2000" report, estimates the risk of an *average* American women being diagnosed with breast cancer:

- at some point before reaching age 40, one in 235
- at some point between age 40 and 59, one in 25
- at some point between age 60 and 79, one in 15

The cancer society provides similar calculations for other types of cancer. It's still good to point out that, for an individual, various factors can mean an above-average or a below-average risk. For example, the *average* person's risk of developing lung cancer has little meaning—unless you get a breakdown for smokers and nonsmokers.

Confusing clusters—Small-scale cancer incidence figures are often deceptive. A town or county may report a startling number of cases of some type of cancer in the area of a chemical plant or toxic waste dump. If you investigate, you may find that many U.S. census tracts or municipalities have equally large numbers just by chance and the laws of statistical variation.

The same applies to that commonly reported phenomenon the *cancer cluster*—an alarming-sounding concentration of some kind of cancer in a city block or neighborhood. In most cases their cause, if any, remains unresolved. Many—some authorities say almost all—are probably the result of statistical variation, in other words, chance. Only in a few cases is some reasonable possible cause, such as an industrial or environmental hot spot, identified.

The difficulty for epidemiologists, reporters, and the public alike is distinguishing possible real problem areas from those that only seem to exist. It takes a large number of new "problem cases" to show up against the normal cancer caseload, and it may take 5 to 40 years' exposure for true problem cases to show up (less for some leukemias).

Case history of a cluster scare: In the mid-1980s, a spate of news stories reported that cancer had been diagnosed in no less than four New York Giants football players. There was public concern about the chemistry (or atmosphere, or something) of the then fairly new New Jersey Meadowlands Sports Complex.

Studies of more than 7,000 people who had worked at the sports complex found that their cancer incidence rate was no higher than the rate in the general population. No dangerous levels of cancer-causing substances were found. And the players' cancers apparently had started before they joined the Giants.

Case closed. From all indications, it was just another coincidence cluster.

How Cancer Figures Are Calculated

Nationwide incidence and survival statistics are estimated by the National Cancer Institute's SEER (Surveillance, Epidemiology and End Results) program. Other groups often use these data to make their own estimates; that probably is the case unless the group credits other more specific and more limited sources.

SEER currently gets its data from area-wide cancer registries in six metropolitan areas (Atlanta, Detroit, San Francisco–Oakland, Los Angeles, San Jose–Monterey, and Seattle–Puget Sound) and five states (Connecticut, Hawaii, Iowa, New Mexico, and Utah). These cover approximately 14 percent of the U.S. population. Extrapolations are then made to get the national incidence and survival figures. (Cancer mortality data are actual counts of death certificates by the government's National Center for Health Statistics.)

The SEER sample has existed in much of its present form only since 1973. This means that all national comparisons with pre-1973 incidence and survival rates are suspect. A former SEER official says, "There are good reasons for believing that substantial subsets of SEER and pre-SEER cancer incidence data are comparable." But some may not be.

Federal health officials will use 2000 population data for a periodic recalculation of some age-adjusted and other age-related health statistics. This will provide better figures but might require adjustments when comparing some new figures with old figures.

We've noted that SEER doesn't count the relatively easy-to-treat forms of skin cancer (but does count melanoma). SEER also doesn't count cases of some in situ cancer-like changes that are so early that they don't fulfill all the usual characteristics of cancer.

You also should know:

- Doctors who treat cancer may report their five-year survival rate even though not all the patients have survived for five years yet.

Example: In 1985, oncologists (cancer doctors) at many centers reported the cumulative results of some newer treatments of breast cancer. Instead of reporting

absolute survival alone—how many patients lived exactly
how long—they used a *life table method* or *actuarial method*.
This allows them to say: Enough of our patients have been
followed for five years, and enough for one, two, three, or
four years, for us to say with confidence what the five-year
survival rate for the whole group will be.

This is considered statistically honest and respectable
if completely described. In fact, one statistician says, "It is
wrong if it is not reported. It is the only way we can know
how we are progressing in this difficult disease." But the
method should be described in our news stories too, to be
honest.

• A cancer researcher sometimes reports patients'
mean or median survival—that is, how long a group
of patients have lived on the average by one of these
measures. The median does tell you that half of the
patients did that well or better. But the measure
picked may be the best-sounding one. Neither mean
nor median tells you how many people have survived
how much longer or how briefly. For that you need
to see a fuller explanation or a revealing table or
graph.

Shifts, Drifts, and Blips

A death blamed on senility in 1900 would probably
have been put down as "general arteriosclerosis" in 1960.
Now it probably would be blamed either on cerebrovascu-
lar disease (including strokes) or Alzheimer's disease,
which only in recent years has been recognized as a cause
of a large proportion of senility and death.

Medical knowledge, medical definitions, doctors'
skills, doctors' diagnostic enthusiasms, and the way statisticians code disease all change. Some diseases—the

connective tissue disorder called lupus and probably cancer of the pancreas—appear to have increased dramatically simply because they are being found more often. Death certificates have been called notoriously inaccurate. The number of autopsies, the most accurate method of identifying cause of death, has dropped sharply in recent years.

These are only a few of the rocks and shoals in determining who died of what and who has what. There are also unexplained or incompletely explained drifts in the statistics, such as the declines in stomach cancer deaths.

The news media also affect disease rates. When reporters write about a particular illness, such as some food-borne malady, more people may see their doctors with such problems, or the patients may report their illnesses directly to health officials.

Then there was the "Betty Ford blip" in breast cancer incidence. This was a dramatic rise in discovery of new cases for a few years after that First Lady's 1974 breast cancer surgery, along with the publicity that her case generated about breast cancer early detection and surgery.

Using the Internet—See "Working the Web" in the Appendix for key web sites for vital statistics and other information.

Health Plans and Hospitals: Measuring Their Quality

8

Ignorance never settles a question.

—Disraeli

"Go on, Mrs. Pratt," says Mrs. Sampson. "Them ideas is so original and soothing. I think statistics are just as lovely as they can be."

—O. Henry

——————— *& & &* ———————

Where can you find a top-quality health plan that you can trust? How can you know one when you see it?

"Quality of care varies enormously," said David Lansky, president of the Foundation for Accountability (FACCT), which promotes the disclosure of medical performance to consumers.[1]

More and more information is becoming available about health maintenance organizations (HMOs) and other managed health plans' performance from the all-important standpoint of what it means for the patients.

Other important data are available on hospitals' performance. And a 1999 study reminds us of the problems that exist. The Institute of Medicine, an arm of the

National Academy of Sciences, analyzed various studies that have looked at medical mistakes, particularly in hospitals, and found grave concerns. The institute concluded that at least 44,000 Americans die each year because of such mistakes.[2]

Serious hospital mistakes most often occur in busy settings such as intensive care units and emergency rooms. But there are other problems as well. One major problem area that's ripe for improvements: medication mix-ups and overdoses. Some are caused by the way drugs are stored in strong concentrations, rather than the diluted forms intended to be given patients. Others are caused when different drugs have confusingly similar names. Still others are caused by some doctors' poor handwriting.

No one is saying that all mistakes could be eliminated in hospitals, where many emergency decisions have to be made in rapid-fire order. And even very small mistakes may be life-threatening for a seriously ill, hospitalized patient. "To err is human, but errors can be prevented," the Institute of Medicine's report said. Or at least errors can be reduced.

Just as with health plans, remember that not all hospitals are equal.

Both the health plan and the hospital data need much care in their interpretation.

Health Plans and Managed Care

Measuring Managed Care

Until the mid-1980s, employers commonly sought data only on health plans' cost. But as managed care plans grew, employers began to seek data on health plans' medical quality, on their service to the plans' members, and on patients' satisfaction. More and more data are becoming publicly available.

A plan's medical "quality" includes the health care that prevents disease (such as immunizations and prenatal care). It includes efforts to catch problems in time for a cure (such as mammograms and Pap smears). It includes data about cholesterol management, other treatments, C-sections, and normal deliveries. It also includes board certification of physicians, patient satisfaction, and accreditation status.

The National Committee for Quality Assurance (NCQA), a nonprofit group with health industry, employer, and consumer members on its board, accredits managed care health plans, and gathers performance data on them. NCQA has the only nationwide health plan statistics that have been subjected to rigorous statistical analysis.

NCQA officials say: "The gap between top and bottom performing plans remains enormous—beta blocker treatment rates [after heart attacks] range from 52 to 92 percent." And, "If all plans were to perform at [NCQA's] 'benchmark' level, it would save tens of thousands of lives annually, reduce costs and significantly reduce illness."[3]

As we enter the 21st century, about three-fourths of the nation's HMOs and similar managed health plans participate in the NCQA program to gather this type of data. But only about three-fourths of the participating plans let NCQA make their results public. Pressure from the news media has the potential to increase the disclosure rate.

Where should interested reporters go from here?

Check with individual health plans, of course. Check with employer groups or labor unions. Check with the NCQA Communications Department in Washington, D.C., or on the Internet at www.ncqa.org. There's a fee for most people who get NCQA data, but exceptions are made for news media.

The American Association of Health Plans, the nation's principal organization representing HMOs and similar managed care plans, is a good contact for information, including a booklet on this subject for reporters (see note 1). The association, based in Washington, D.C., strongly supports public dissemination about health plans' performance.

In some people's mind, HMOs and managed care plans are synonymous. But managed care is a broader term. It includes HMOs, which require that virtually all medical care be received through participating doctors and hospitals. And it includes other types of managed care plans (preferred provider plans, etc.) that provide financial incentives for patients to use participating health care providers but still allow some coverage when members use other providers. Keep these differences in mind when making comparisons.

Reporters often want to do their own analysis of data—or even gather their own data. But there are some advantages in using industry and NCQA data, such as standardized categories for easier plan-to-plan comparisons. Reporters should use extra care as they venture into their own data collection.

As you begin to gather and analyze data from plans, from NCQA and from other sources:

1. To measure quality of care, use numbers that avoid subjective judgments. Use solid numbers such as the percentage of patients who have had a particular type of cancer early-detection exam, or who have received specialized care for a particular medical condition.

Theoretically, it would be even better to find out how many people get successful treatments for cancer or for other problems. That type of data is beginning to come. But if this type of data is used, "success" must be clearly and carefully defined.

2. To measure satisfaction, ask the right patients.
Various polls (conducted by health plans as well as the news media), ask: "Are you satisfied with your health plan?" Or "Are you satisfied with your doctor?" Some people may answer "yes" when they've been well and haven't used their health plans recently. Stratify the data to see how the people who used their health plans the most answer these questions.

3. All patients aren't the same. Ask: Is your plan's score higher simply because its members are younger and therefore not sick as often? Check to see whether statistics that make plan-to-plan comparisons have been "age adjusted" or adjusted for other factors.

Detailed analysis is a job for an expert, usually a medical statistician. If health plans and other industry sources do their own data collection and analysis, ask: Who was your statistician? If you do your own data collection and analysis, consult an expert at a university or major teaching hospital.

4. Remember the healthy-worker effect. Here's how this can come into play when you compare health plans' statistics with overall state or national statistics:

Many health care plans enroll only, or mostly, employed people—and often those in above-minimum-wage jobs. As a result, a health plan may have relatively few low-income people, relatively few disabled people, and relatively few people from other disadvantaged groups. For various reasons, these are people who tend to have more medical problems.

Low-income, disabled, and other disadvantaged people can lower the overall health-outcomes data for the entire state or nation. This can make the health plan's membership look very healthy by comparison, whether the health plan is doing a good job or not. So use care in making comparisons.

5. Don't expect 100 percent success rates. *Example:* Some women refuse mammograms, or fail to show up to have them. If a plan does report a 100 percent success rate of getting patients to undergo screening (or to get vaccines, or to take other preventive steps), be suspicious rather than automatically laudatory.

Some reported rates should be low or relatively low, like hospital readmissions for some conditions.

6. Focus on the right age group or other subpopulations. If you are asking about mammograms, for example, ask women in older age groups, for whom annual mammograms are recommended. If you are asking about the rate of pregnancy counseling, the best information would be women ages 19 to 28, who have the highest birth rates.

7. Don't forget costs. And in comparing costs between health plans, don't forget patients' out-of-pocket payments. Plans differ on copayments that patients must pay for some services. Plans cover prescription drugs to varying extents. Consider all in making comparisons.

8. Ask *why* patients and doctors are leaving health plans. Statistics on patient and physician disenrollments (the industry term) can be analyzed for signs of dissatisfaction. But don't jump to conclusions. Physicians may leave a health plan for various reasons. Patients may be moved from one plan to another by employers seeking lower rates.

9. Ask, ask, ask. Ask health plan officials why they score low in certain areas. And ask what they are doing right to score high, when they do.

Ask your state's insurance commissioner's office and your state health department what data do they have on complaints to them about health plans. Talk to doctors. Talk to other experts.

And talk to patients. A health plan may have good overall quality-of-care scores but may have gaps in care to specific types of patients.

10. In doing all this, don't forget the rest of this book.

Beware of small numbers. *Examples:* Small subgroups, such as only boys in a narrow age group who visit a particular pediatric clinic. Or a poll with a small number of people interviewed.

Beware of small differences, which may be due to chance alone.

And beware of possible apples-to-oranges comparisons. *Example:* Two plans show a difference in five-year survival among breast cancer patients. Are the two groups of patients matched in age and stage of disease?

Managed Care: Presenting Your Findings

Don't give a free ride to uncooperative health plans. Plans that refuse to provide quality-of-care and other data may be doing worse than the lowest scoring plans that do provide data. Give credit to plans that provide their figures. Point out—sharply and clearly—the plans that don't.

Some private-office (fee-for-service) doctors operate on their own, outside managed care plans. These physicians are unlikely to have the type of medical-practice statistics that managed care plans are beginning to provide. Point this out to your readers or viewers.

Focus on what you think is most important for your readers or viewers. Overall scores don't tell the full story.

A plan may be good at some things, not at others. What you think is most important for your readers or viewers is likely to include prevention. It also may include care of children, women, the elderly, or the chronically ill.

Do for your readers what you expect health plans to do for you. When you analyze quality of care or cost data, tell your readers your methodology. Tell them your survey plan, and your ways of adding up numbers to arrive at judgments. Also, consider sharing your methodology with health plans while you are asking them for data. This may help you get valid, apples-to-apples comparisons between plans.

Don't drop a good story. Check back with a low-scoring health plan a few months later to ask its officials what they have done to improve. Check back with all health plans when new figures are available, to see how they do over time.

Hospital Care Statistics

Measuring Hospitals' Care

Hospitalized patients' fates, good or bad, are called *outcomes*. And outcome rates are increasingly important in assessing both the medical and the cost effectiveness of health care. They can include improvement, recovery, cure, failure (the patient didn't get well), complications, disability, survival, and mortality rates.

Various data comparing individual hospitals are available from some state agencies, from some hospitals, from some employers who gather data to aid in their section of health insurance plans, and from other sources.

These figures do need interpretation. Take hospital death rates, for example. We may get them for all hospitals or just for *outliers*. These are hospitals with rates well

above or below expected or predicted rates based on
national averages. But these rates alone still may not tell
you which hospitals may be lifesavers and which may be
death traps.

The rates may have been adjusted for some variables—such as age, gender, previous hospitalization, and
the presence of various co-morbidities (illnesses other
than the main one causing the admission)—to try to make
one hospital's rates comparable with another's. But they
may not have been adequately adjusted for the most
important variable of all, severity of illness. Very likely,
they also haven't been adjusted for other aspects of
patient mix, perhaps including socio-economic status and
other characteristics that can affect medical outcomes.

For this reason, a mere list of hospitals and mortality
rates will not tell you that hospital A's patients may be far
sicker than hospital B's. Or poorer, which generally means
sicker. Or homeless or without family or other resources,
so they cannot readily be transferred to a nursing home or
hospice or their own homes and thus often die in the hospital. Or hospital A's patients may to a larger extent be
emergency admissions, which also means sicker. A trauma
center, a hospital that specializes in burns, and a tertiary-
care center where other hospitals send their most complicated cases all may have higher death rates than a simpler
community hospital.

Experience so far shows that virtually every hospital
official, confronted with a report of high death rates, will
say, "Our patients are sicker." But many studies show that
there are true differences in care from hospital to hospital.

Hospital Quality: Questions to Ask

The first question to ask anyone (and to ask yourself
while looking at the figures) is: How can any of these

statistics be of use to patients? Do any of these numbers show anything that a potential patient should know?

When you are told that a hospital's patients are different, poorer or sicker, or more emergency room cases, and that this explains poorer outcomes, ask:

Can you back that up with statistics, including statistics about this hospital's population compared with those of other hospitals in the area?

Can you point to any hospital with similar patient mixes that has equally unfavorable-sounding rates, in or out of your area?

What about these figures that show that some other hospitals in the same class—X University Hospital and Y City Hospital—manage to treat tough patients and keep their death rate down?

"Bad-apple" physicians, not the hospital, are frequently responsible for bad outcomes. Ask a hospital's officials: Do any of the surgeons have mortality rates that are prompting the hospital to take any action? An equivocal answer or "no comment" may be revealing.

If you ask about a specific procedure, such as coronary bypass surgery, you may be told that a hospital's high mortality does not mean it isn't giving superior care. Ask: Is this hospital doing enough of these procedures to be one of the most experienced and successful hospitals? Or is it treating so few patients of this kind that its physicians and staff can't possibly get enough experience to be among the most skilled?

Dr. Sidney Wolfe, director of the Health Research Group founded by Ralph Nader, discussed a federal Health Care Financing Administration (HCFA) release of a small number of hospital mortality rates in March 1986:

Of 33 hospitals with an elevated coronary bypass mortality rate, 24 were doing fewer than 100 operations a year. The lowest mortality rate among them was 14 percent. "That's just unconscionable," Wolfe said.

Conversely the hospitals with lower-than-expected mortality rates, all under 2 percent (a rate seven times lower), did more than 300 bypass operations each year on Medicare patients alone. "What this tells us is that hospitals that are doing very few of these operations, or any others, shouldn't be doing them at all," Wolfe concluded.

Researchers came up with a broader estimate in the March 2000 issue of the *Journal of the American Medical Association*. About 4,000 lives a year might be saved nationwide if surgical patients used only hospitals that had high volumes for selective types of surgery, based on other statistical studies linking volume to mortality rates. But more study is needed to confirm all such estimates, both the research report (which focused on California surgical patterns) and an accompanying editorial (which took the national perspective) cautioned.[4]

If you are told that the mortality rate is high because the hospital has a policy of not sending patients home to die unless they have family and home resources, ask:

How can this hospital afford to do that in the face of insurance limits that often reimburse the hospital for an average number of days of care? Don't many hospitals succeed in transferring such patients to a hospice or a nursing home? Does this say something about the hospital's need for improvement in its social services, or discharge planning, or cooperation with other community resources?

If you are still troubled about a hospital's mortality rate, ask yourself, ask doctors, ask others:

Would you go to this hospital or send someone in your family there?

And ask hospital officials: Has your hospital studied the situation by examining your medical or surgical practices? Has the hospital made any changes, or will it at least be thinking about changes? This could include changes in medical staff privileges (who can do what kind of surgery), among other things.

Even when a hospital has a low mortality rate, ask: Do you credit this to superior care, or the fact that this hospital primarily attracts an economically upscale, relatively healthy population?

As with health plans, don't forget the rest of the book in assessing hospitals. The laws of chance and variability mean that differences may not be significant when small numbers are involved. Still, don't let that dissuade you from asking questions. Check back after a few months to ask a low-scoring hospital what it has done to improve. Check back when new numbers are available to see how all hospitals do over time.

Health costs—For a surprising way that prevention can affect health costs, see "More About Money: The Stop-Smoking Paradox" in Chapter 11.

Our Environment and Measuring All Risks

9

 & & &

One expert says, "The hazard is horrendous." Another,
"The hazard is minimal or nonexistent."

Not only do experts disagree about environmental
issues, but sometimes they are part of the problem, says
Baruch Fischhoff, professor of engineering and public
policy at Carnegie Mellon University in Pittsburgh.[1]

"For example, Three Mile Island, Bhopal and Exxon
Valdez* hit the news because the engineers who designed
those systems made unrealistic assumptions about how
hard it would be to operate them," Fischhoff says.

A more recent example is the 1999 nuclear plant accident in Tokaimura, Japan, which was triggered by workers
who accidentally overloaded a container with uranium.
This caused an uncontrolled atomic reaction that sent
radioactive particles into the air, forcing thousands of

people to stay indoors. Slow-to-react government experts called what happened "inconceivable."

Hazardous waste incinerators provoke protests because their promoters don't think to involve affected residents in the site-selection process, Fischhoff says. "The chemists and entomologists [insect experts] who formulated DDT knew and thought little about the fragility of birds' eggs, which was another profession's department," he adds.

Too often, "journalists must assemble the pieces of a story whose contours are only gradually emerging to the people involved," Fischhoff concludes. So reporters may need to talk not only to experts on both sides of an issue, but to experts in diverse fields. Other challenges for reporters:

- **Reporters may need to act swiftly when environmental issues affect people's health.** "Public health has never clung to the principle that complete knowledge about a potential health hazard is a prerequisite for action," says an editorial in the *American Journal of Public Health.*[2]
- **The data on an environmental issue may be incomplete, or nonexistent.**
- **The public views different risks in different ways.** Much of the public doesn't worry greatly about driving, using seat belts, drinking, or smoking. But the public often vibrates about such lesser and less certain dangers as chemicals in our foods. Someone said, "Americans want to be protected from nuclear accidents so they can go hang gliding."

It's not entirely illogical. We decide for ourselves whether to accept the risk of driving, drinking, or mountain climbing. It's easier to cope with the known than with the unknown and the mysteriously threatening. We may feel very different about a risk that someone imposed on us—or a risk that grows larger than believed at first.

While this chapter focuses primarily on environmental issues, the basic principles of risk reporting apply to many other areas as well. There are 18 specific tips for risk reporting at the end of this chapter.

Start with Some Key Questions

An oil spill covers beaches with black sludge and bodies of birds. A community, puzzled over some strange illnesses, discovers it is sitting on a toxic waste dump. Many of these events do not injure large numbers of people, as far as we can tell. Yet thousands are scared or concerned. We have been told too often that something is safe, only to learn later that this assurance was wrong or that the uncovering of new data changes the picture. Waterways have been polluted; men and women have been fatally exposed in the workplace. There are toxic waste dumps. There is acid rain.

There are TV news specials and big headlines. The news media may be accused of overstating, needlessly alarming, emphasizing the worst possible case, reporting unsupported conclusions—or being falsely reassuring. Stung by the criticism, we reporters may write "on the one hand, on the other hand" stories, which don't help our readers or viewers figure out if one hand is holding the most creditable evidence. What's a reporter to do?**

Based on what both scientific experts and veteran reporters say, reporters need to get answers—to the extent known—to these basic questions about environmental (and often other) risks:

1. What's the risk? Is it great or small?
2. Under what circumstances?

3. How certain—or uncertain—is this? If the evidence is strong, give specifics. If the studies are weak, say so. If no one knows, say so. Don't hesitate to say "might" or "is believed to." Needed qualifiers can add creditability to a report.

4. What can be done to reduce any risk? This may include personal actions, or a new law or regulations, or better enforcement of existing regulations, or changes in business or farm practices, or some other actions. Or a combination of these things.

5. What are the alternatives? Are there any benefits from the substance that is posing the risk? Who benefits? How do they benefit? How do you weigh the benefits versus the risks? Would avoiding one risk introduce other problems?

Also: The risks to our environment aren't limited to risks to human health or animals' well-being. We all enjoy clean air and water, so that alone is an excellent reason to keep them clean. But we reporters should make clear, to our readers and viewers, what types of risks and concerns we are talking about.

How do you get the answers to these five questions?

You can start by asking people who are claiming environmental risks:

- What are your specific claims?
- What's your scientific evidence?
- Does the evidence meet statistical and other scientific tests? If it can't meet scientific standards (e.g., if the findings might be due to chance alone), why do you think action should be taken anyway?

You can address equally important questions to people who downgrade or deny a risk (the following are based on a checklist prepared by Dr. Peter Montague at Princeton University):[3]

- When you are told about "safe averages," remember that we encounter hazards as individuals or groups. If an industrial plant releases a toxic substance, the most important thing is not the average amount that gets in the air, but the amount downwind of the plant where people will breathe it. Ask: What does this mean to individuals? To your community?
- When you are told there is "no immediate threat," ask: Is there any delayed hazard? Cancer and some other problems may develop years later.
- When you are told "there is no evidence of hazard," ask: Has anyone made any scientific studies?
- When you are told a hazard is "negligible" or "nonhazardous," ask: What would you do? Would you eat or drink it? Would you raise your children in its presence? What do you think the public should do?
- When you are told about a risk-benefit or cost-benefit analysis, ask: Who bears the risk? Who pays the costs? Who gets the benefit? Have those who will bear the risk given their informed consent?

Evaluate What You've Learned

It's good to have a show-me attitude when anyone presents you with risk-related data.

Watch the risk numbers. To influence us, someone can choose an annual death toll, or deaths per thousand or million people, or per-thousand persons exposed. Or we may be given deaths per ton of some substance, or per ton released into the air, or per facility. If you think a different figure is more appropriate, ask for it. Or ask the other side in a controversy what figure it thinks is most appropriate.

Dr. Thomas M. Vogt offered another example, this time about a nonenvironmental risk: A researcher said widows constituted 15 percent, but widowers only 5

percent, of the 400 suicides in a California county over a
four-year period, "suggesting that males better tolerate
the loss of their marital partners." Census data—not
included in the state medical journal article—showed that
there were five times as many widows as widowers in the
county. As a result, the suicide *rate* (suicides per thousand
people) was actually *lower* for widows than for widowers.[4]

Be suspicious of sweeping claims such as "substance
A causes everything from ingrown toenails to cancer."
Substances can have multiple effects, but broad statements are very suspicious until proven otherwise. It's
more likely that substance A causes disease B—although
that too must be supported by evidence.

Look at risk-related scientific evidence with the same
careful eye that we have discussed in the earlier chapters.
Experts point to these important things to remember in
dealing with environmental risks:

Pay attention to the strength of an association. If
exposure to substance A seems to make your chance of
getting cancer 1.5 times as likely, that translates into a
high-sounding 50 percent excess risk. But given the limi-
tation of human data, it may or may not be a real risk. By
comparison, we know that smoking is a big risk. The risk
of lung cancer is 10 times higher in smokers than in nonsmokers. See "Putting Numbers on Risks" in Chapter 7.

Always, look at *all* the numbers. How sure or unsure
are you that the data are reliable and statistically sound?
Look for statistical significance, which means there's only
a small possibility that the same results could have been
achieved by chance alone. See "How Probable Is It?" in
Chapter 3 and the questions you can ask about probability in Chapter 5. Even when the data have been carefully
collected and meet the statistical tests of probability, you
must . . .

Look for alternative explanations. Could the healthy-
worker effect have made a workplace (or other situation)

look safer than it really is? You look at the workers exposed to substance A, find that they are actually healthier than the general population, and exonerate the substance—possibly wrongly.

Workers tend to be healthier and live longer than the population in general; they have to be healthy to get their jobs and then to keep working. So workers should be compared with their peers—for example, workers in a related industry or in another department.

On the other hand, could an above-average rate of cigarette smoking by workers be responsible for their problems, rather than some suspect chemical in the workplace? See Chapter 3 ("Eliminate Bias; Consider Alternate Explanations") for a detailed discussion of other explanations.

Recognize the true complexity of environmental problems. Almost every environmental or chemical effect on people or their surroundings involves many interactions between many factors, often at many times and places, and often involving various chemicals.

So more and more scientists are skeptical of studying risk by looking at only one chemical at a time. We live with many chemicals in the air, in what we eat and drink, and in all sorts of things that we use. The combined risks may be what's important.

And there are other complexities that may need to be considered. Take, for example, relationship between pollution and cancer. Here are some questions to ask in probing the complexity of this issue:

What kinds of pollutants are we talking about? What kinds of cancer? Are there multiple causes? Are there interactions between causes? Who is exposed? Is everyone equally vulnerable? Do they also smoke or have exposures to other carcinogens?

Are there other possible explanations? Are the numbers large enough to be reliable? Are there enough cases to show up—that is, to be distinguished from other cancers occurring for other reasons? Since cancer often has a long latency period, will we have to wait 20 or 30 years to find out?

Give added weight to research that has been replicated. Research that has been repeated by different research groups that have reached basically the same conclusion each time is more reliable. But you still must . . .

Accept some uncertainty. The greenhouse effect (carbon dioxide buildup and the resulting warming of the atmosphere caused by our burning fossil fuels) and the effects of acid rain, of fluorocarbons on the ozone layer, and of nuclear waste disposal also will take decades to assess. In many cases—for example, radioactivity at Hiroshima and Agent Orange and dioxide in Vietnam—exposure levels are unknown. In most cases, true human trials (controlled exposure of human subjects to some pollutant) are ethically impossible.

"Acute diseases are fairly easy to measure," one environmental scientist says. "But chronic diseases—say, nervous system effects or effects on the fetus—are devilishly hard to recognize with precision, and they may take 20 years to show up. So we use a looser and looser screen and end up with many false positives."[5]

The bottom line: There may be neither overwhelming evidence for or against a direct cause and effect, nor any way of easy prediction or quick solution. As the Conservation Foundation has put it, "When the weather forecaster is vague about how much it will snow tomorrow, if at all, how can we expect scientists to calculate how many degrees the Earth will warm up in 40 years because of carbon dioxide loading?"[6]

"There is never enough data," Michael Greenberg at Rutgers University says. "I tend to have more belief in the individual who admits data weakness."

Questions you can ask about some of the points in this section appear under "Questions to Evaluate Studies" later in this chapter.

Know the Limits of Science

Science can't prove a negative. No study can ever prove that something is not harmful, or that something does not exist—even though that's just what the public often wants to hear. It's useless to ask, "Can you guarantee that X doesn't cause male pattern baldness," because there no scientific way to prove that it couldn't.

As one statistician explains, probability "practically guarantees that a small number of studies will show some 'statistically significant' findings if enough studies are carried out. As a result, we can never be 100 percent sure that the null hypothesis of no-association . . . is true."[7]

On the other hand, it's still fair to cite the lack of evidence that a problem exists. But avoid words like "proof." And careful studies can go a long way in calming controversies about new technologies as well as about environmental chemical concerns.

Case history: A Florida man, appearing on a major TV talk show in 1993, triggered a national debate by claiming that his wife's brain cancer was caused by the cell phone that he had given her. Some studies do indicate that microwaves (which cell phones emit) might damage nearby tissue. Other scientists question these findings, and epidemiologists note that brain cancer incidence has not risen nationally. In late 2000, two rigorous studies found that cell-phone users were no more likely than other people to develop brain cancer. Typical of careful comment by experts, these two studies are "the best information to date, and they provide much reassurance."[8] But with cell phones still a relatively new technology, more studies involving longer-term use may still be needed.

Humans can't be treated like laboratory rats. It would be unethical to expose people, in a controlled experiment, to a chemical expected to cause cancer or some other serious problem. Scientists can, of course, use other methods. For example, they can make comparisons with historical data, which is sometimes inaccurate. They can use animal experiments, recognizing that no animal is a perfect substitute for humans. They can use case-control studies, comparing affected people and healthy people. But as valuable as these methods are, they all have limits, as described in earlier chapters.

Dose response doesn't follow a single set of rules. Looking at the results of a study—almost always the results of a sample, since few studies cover everybody in a population—a scientist must try to extrapolate or project or infer to a larger or another population. For instance, she or he must try to extrapolate the effects of a high dose of a substance to someone who gets a low dose.

To do so, the scientist needs to ask: Am I dealing with a *linear* relationship? That would be, say, one in which a dose of 0.01 has a ten-thousandth of the effect of a dose of 100? Or is this a *nonlinear relationship* in which there is a threshold at some point, below which low doses have no effect and are safe?

Some relationships in nature are indeed linear, and even more are linear only in part, or definitely nonlinear. But a scientist pondering the effects of fumes of some chemical may not know which relationship applies. What he usually has in hand are data from exposures to high doses in humans or animals or both. The scientist may be asked to help make a practical decision on whether low doses are safe or dangerous.

The scientist might assume there is no threshold and there is indeed a risk from a very small dose. In order to be certain that everyone is protected, the plant might be closed. But this could pose job loss and other problems.

Or the scientist might assume that there is a threshold and that low doses are probably safe. If the plant remains open, then some people might be harmed by the doses of fumes that they inhale.

The bottom line: In cases like these, the decisions are policy decisions, not scientific ones. Scientists can only contribute the best possible data to assist the policymakers in determining which possible risks are acceptable and which are not. Journalists should tell their readers and viewers what is science and what is policymaking, and what is unknown as well as what is known.

"Risk-benefit assessment" has special limits. *Risk assessment* is often a necessary way of using studies, facts, and conjectures to make a practical assessment of risk, whether the risk of PCBs (polychlorinated biphenyls) or of not installing air bags in our cars.

Risk assessment often gets stepped up to *risk-benefit assessment*—weighing both the probable bad and the probable good. The risk-benefit process involves not only science but psychology, culture, ideology, economics, values, and politics.

Other things make this tricky as well. How do you put a cost on a human life, or even on a pretty hilltop view? In deciding on the location for a waste disposal plant, how do we weigh the concerns of the small number of people who may live near the site with the much larger number of people whose wastes will fill the site?

Nevertheless, risk-benefit assessment can get all facts and uncertainties out on the table for public consideration. Despite the potential problems, you can tell your readers what's known and what's unknown about environmental risks, controversies, and studies. The next two sections contain questions you can ask to get the answers you need.

Questions to Evaluate Hazards

Dr. Peter Montague and others offer specific suggestions and questions to help evaluate environmental and chemical hazards. (The language in this section is in largest part, but not entirely, Montague's.) First, how big is the hazard . . .

Compared with background levels—A rule of thumb (not always true, but a good guideline to decide whether something deserves serious investigation): A 10 percent increase above natural background levels is something to pay attention to. A factor-of-2 increase (a doubling) should be of real concern. A factor-of-10 increase is big; a factor-of-100 increase, very big.

In comparing hazards to their background levels—which is important to do whenever possible—remember that these levels are not necessarily totally safe. Background radiation and natural toxins in food may have some effect on humans. But they are usually the least hazardous we can expect.

Compared with standards for workers—If there is no natural background level, look for federal or state standards for workers. It is common to assume that the general public will be adequately protected by a contamination level 10 to 100 times lower than that permitted in the workplace.

The public also, of course, includes infants, the elderly, the chronically ill, urbanites who breathe a mixture of many contaminants, and many people who are more sensitive than others. Thus the reasoning that the public will be protected by a standard 10 to 100 times tighter than a workplace standard has its limits, but it is probably sound as a general rule in the absence of information to the contrary.

Compared with other standards—Are there drinking water standards or air standards? Given such a standard, you can calculate how much water or air would be needed to dilute a substance to acceptable standards.

Example: A company was dumping only 10 gallons of trichloroethylene onto the ground a year—"really no problem," the company said, though it reached the groundwater. The federal criterion for this chemical is 2.7 parts per billion (ppb), or micrograms per liter. It would take more than 3.5 billion gallons of water to dilute 10 gallons to this level. At an average per capita fluid consumption of two quarts a day, 3.5 billion gallons is enough drinking water for 19 million people for a year. So this kind of analysis can tell you that 10 gallons of trichloroethylene reaching an underground aquifer is not a small problem.

It's useful to know that a human's daily fluid intake averages two quarts, and the average human breathes 23 cubic meters of air daily.

If state and federal standards exist but are in conflict, give both. The public debate will be heated up, all to the good.

What if no standards exist, the case 9 times out of 10? You can only ask a series of fundamental questions of experts (or reference books) and try to put together a best guess.

Now some questions to pin down specific risks—and to assess possible actions:

How does the material behave?—Is this material toxic? How does it get into the environment? Is it vented into the air, discharged into sewage systems, disposed of as wastes?

Is it soluble in water? If so, it tends to be mobile—the world is a wet place. What water supplies could this contamination reach? What towns take their water from this water supply? What's the effect on drinking water?

Is it soluble in lipids—fatty tissue—like DDT is? This makes our bodies repositories.

Will it enter food chains and concentrate? We're at the top of many chains.

Is it likely to become airborne as a gas or dust? Will it then go into the lungs and pass into the bloodstream?

Will it break down—biodegrade—in the environment, or stay around a long time? How long? Are any of its breakdown products also toxic?

If you can learn or determine a lethal dose (LD) or toxic dose, divide it into the total amount of the substance involved to determine the total number of doses you're dealing with.

What are the substance's hazards to the environment other than the human health impact? Can it migrate to ground water and cause a bad taste? Can it kill fish, birds, insects, or plants (other than its target species, if a pesticide or herbicide)? What studies have been done to gauge this?

You can ask: Would you eat or drink substance A? What are you doing about it? What do you think the public should do?

To those who say, "We don't know the answers," ask: Are you going to try to find out? Is a study planned, by you or by others?

Who's responsible?—When there is an accident or an environmental or other chemical problem, ask: Who has the legal responsibility for compensation, for a cleanup, for a solution? What is going to be done immediately—or as soon as possible—to decontaminate or try to control this problem? How is exposure—in the workplace, in the general environment—to be controlled in the future? Keep in mind that quick fixes aren't always the best fixes.

When someone says, "This solution will be state-of-the-art, the very best technology can do," that may be true. But ask: Is this an adequate solution—for public health and safety and for protection of the environment?

Is the solution workable? Have the management and operation been well thought out? Has human error been anticipated? Will there be continuous monitoring for some unexpected release?

What will happen if someone makes a serious error? To quote columnist Ellen Goodman, "We are stuck here in the high-tech, high-risk world with our own low-tech species."

Group versus individual risk—Someone says don't worry, a toxic waste disposal site is being built in a rural area where few people live. True, fewer people will be affected if a chemical brew leaks from the site. But for an individual who lives near the site, regardless of where the site is, the risk remains the same.

We add these possible questions to ask—from various experts—for two specific types of hazards, pesticides and radiation:

Pesticides—Has a federal tolerance, or maximum permitted residue, been set for this product? What foods does it cover? What information was used to set the tolerance? Has use increased since the tolerance was set? Is the tolerance still adequate? Are there recent studies of actual residue in food?

Radiation—In reporting on radiation (whether it's on the Three Mile Island scale or something smaller but still worrisome), distinguish between the radiation that has actually reached people and any radioactive fallout in the air, water, soil, crops, and milk. Ask:

What are the fallout levels in the air, water, and soil? How much has reached or may reach food supplies?

What chemical elements are involved? (Radioactive iodine, plutonium, etc., may enter and affect the body in different ways.)

What is the current or expected whole-body exposure? How much is a lethal dose—one causing imminent death? How much is a harmful dose? From the standpoint of cancer? Of future birth defects? Of early death?

How do the radiation levels compare with the area's natural background—the radioactivity always present in air, water, soil, and rocks? A comparison with background levels may sometimes reveal almost no added increment. But be aware that, in one environmentalist's words, "this is a time-honored way to minimize adverse effects."

Questions to Evaluate Studies

The general advice in previous chapters applies to environmental studies and other claims. But some environmentally tailored questions may help. Pick and choose those that you need to ask a researcher, officials, or someone else for a particular article or situation.

The basics—What is your evidence? What do you base your conclusions on? What type of study have you done (or what study are you citing in support of your views)? Have other experts reviewed it?

The numbers—When you are told about rates and excess risks: What are the actual figures? How many people are affected out of how large a population? What sort of rate would you expect normally? What are the rates elsewhere?

Are your assumptions based on human or animal data?

If human data—How many people have you looked at? Are your study groups large enough to give you confidence that your conclusions are correct?

Sampling—Do you believe your sample (the people studied) is representative of the general population? Or of the population you're trying to apply it to? How did you pick your sample? At random?

Keep in mind that volunteers may be people with a gripe.

Example: A questionnaire, sent to a large group of women, asked them if they had received breast implants and how their health was. Only a fraction of the women returned the questionnaire. But among those who did, a surprisingly large number had breast implants. And they reported a large number of health problems. Some experts took the survey's results to mean that the implants were very unsafe. Other experts countered that women who had a gripe about their implants were more likely to have taken the time to return the questionnaire. Other studies have done a better job of sorting out which problems probably are, and which problems probably aren't, caused by breast implants. But the debate continues.

Cases—If conclusions are based on cases—people supposedly affected by some agent: Have you yourself observed the effects in the people you're talking about, or did you have to depend on their recall?

We noted in Chapter 4 that some people attribute normal aches, pains, and stomach growls to whatever infectious illness is in the news. Similarly, a neighborhood discovers that it rests on a toxic waste dump, and people say, "That's why I've been sick!" A human enough reaction, sometimes right, often wrong. Only careful study can link such complaints to some environment problem.

Some people may even worry themselves sick. There is debate over whether some war-related illnesses fit into this category, although other cases are no doubt real.

At the extreme, there are rare yet intriguing outbreaks of *epidemic hysteria.* In Washington, D.C., some barrels that were mislabeled "Hazard—Radioactive" rolled off a truck. Even though there was no radiation, the workers cleaning up the mess began feeling ill. In McMinnville, Tennessee, a teacher reported that she smelled a gasoline odor. Eighty students and 19 staff members then felt sick enough to go to a hospital emergency room, where doctors could find nothing wrong.[9]

Of course, this is no reason for you to dismiss all claims of illness. But these weird outbreaks are a reminder that, at times, the power of suggestion can be powerful.

To gauge toxicity: Was everyone who was exposed affected? Usually this is not the case; when it is, it may indicate an unusually high level of toxicity. Do you have any information on the people's exposure?

If the reported illnesses are serious: Did you examine the people reportedly affected? Who made what diagnoses? Were the diagnoses firm? Do you have any information on their exposures?

Limits and doubts—How certain are you? What is really known and what is still unknown? What is the degree of uncertainty? Are you missing any data you would like to have?

Could the association or result have occurred just by chance? What are your figures for statistical significance? Check the *P* value or confidence level. (See "How Probable Is It?" in Chapter 3.)

Are you concluding that there is a cause-and-effect relationship? Or only a possible suspicious association?

What possible weaknesses or qualifications still apply to your findings or conclusions? Could something else— any other variables, any biases, anything else—have accounted for your results? You should look favorably on a researcher's clear, forthright statement on such matters, unless the defects are overwhelming.

Exposures and dosages—Have you found a dose-response relationship? How much of this substance causes how much harm? Or is the answer "We don't know"?

Are you assuming there is an effect at a low dose because you believe there is a linear relationship—and no threshold or cutoff—between low and known high doses? Or is there some other reason for your extrapolation?

Do people in your field agree that this relationship is right for this chemical (or whatever)?

Who in the population does it apply to? What's the extent of the risk? Can you say what it means to individuals?

Is the risk a definite number or rate, or is there a range of possibilities, depending on your assumptions or differing interpretations of your data?

Is the risk cited for current exposure levels, or for some projected future levels? Is the risk based on the amount of contaminated food that an average person eats, or on the large amounts that only some people eat? Are there individual sensitivities?

Are there alternatives to this chemical (or other agent), and what do we know about their risks?

Animal tests—Have animal studies been done on this chemical? Were they long-term studies (such as two-year or longer bioassays for cancer) or short-term (six months or so). Short-term studies yield quick results but are not as good as long-term studies.

Were studies conducted for mutagenicity and reproductive effects as well as for cancer? How many species were tested? Usually it's mice and rats.

What was the method of exposure? Inhalation? Feeding? Skin exposure (dermal)? Something in our food supply might best be tested by a feeding study; a workplace exposure, by skin exposure. See "Animals as Stand-Ins for Us" in Chapter 6 for more information on animal studies.

A fit with other findings?—What do other experts think? Are there other studies or conclusions that bear out what you say? Can you cite specific ones I can look up?

Critics' views—What do your critics say? Who are they? Then you may ask the critics, among other things: Have I been asking the right questions?

Researchers' views—Some scientists have strongly felt political, social, or economic connections, and they might not reveal them to you unless you ask. This does not mean their work or assertions should not be judged on their own merits. Almost everyone is connected to something and has opinions and biases.

Still, you can ask: What are your personal values on this subject? Have you taken public stands on this issue? Do you belong to any organization that has taken similar positions? What government agencies, or companies, or other groups have supported your research?

If questioning a member of a political administration who is stating some conclusion or policy, ask or find out: What is the administration's policy on this? Is your conclusion the same? Have people outside the government come to the same conclusion?

Opinions, connections, and sources of financing are normally not indictments. The public still has a right to know them.

Some scientists on all sides—industry, government, environmental groups—"make sweeping judgments on the basis of incomplete, and hence inadequate, data," emphasize their own views, and suppress or minimize conflicting evidence, a Twentieth Century Fund task force concluded.[10]

Yet keep in mind these words from Dr. Gary Friedman: "Ultimately we must all rely on the integrity and objective of the researcher, and the basic scientific process of repetition of studies by other investigators."[11]

Special Statistical Situations

Some other things to keep in mind as you ask questions:

Synergistic effect—This occurs when two things work together to create unexpectedly large effects. Smokers exposed to asbestos fibers, for example, have an unusually high rate of lung cancer. The federal National Cancer

Institute offers these figures on its web site, *www.nci.nih.gov:*

Cigarette smokers, on the average, are 10 times more likely to develop lung cancer than nonsmokers. For nonsmokers who work with asbestos, the risk is about five times greater than for people in the general population. "By contrast, smokers who are heavily exposed to asbestos are as much as 90 times more likely to develop lung cancer than are non-exposed individuals who do not smoke."

Scaling up—Inappropriate scaling can produce two common errors made by both journalists and analysts:

- You see 2 or 3 or 20 cases of a disease and assume that the results apply to a larger population. This is the *individualistic fallacy.* Your sample must be large enough, and representative enough, before you may reliably and validly extrapolate.
- You study 10 cities along the Ohio River and find a relationship between water quality and reported bladder cancer. You assume there is probably a cause-and-effect relationship. And you assume that the same is probably true anyplace with the same water quality, and individuals or groups of individuals in other cities with similar water quality must be victims of the same problem. You may be engaging in the *ecological fallacy.* If you studied 100 towns with the same kind of water or did a careful comparison of bladder cancer patients with comparable controls, you might find that something entirely different caused the cancers.

Another way of counting—One more term that you may encounter in some types of studies: *nonparametric methods.* These are methods of examining data that do not rely on a numerical distribution. As a result, they don't allow a few very large or very small or very wild numbers to run away with the analysis.

Example: Using just plus or minus signs rather than specific counts for reactions to a substance or a medical treatment. You count up and compare the number of pluses and minuses. Or you might group your counts by rank from least to greatest.

These methods can sometimes be valuable—when used with care. Ask the researcher why this approach was used; look for a reasoned answer.

Tips for Reporting Risks

Here are suggestions, from top reporters and from others, to use in reporting and writing about environmental and other risks:

1. **Use caution in writing "safe."** We hear of safe drugs, safe cars, environmental safety, safety caps. Then comes a drug recall, or someone dying of unexpected side effects from what was thought to be a "breakthrough" drug. Or a manufacturer's recall of cars, for safety sake. Things are seldom completely safe. Often we should say, "this means relatively safe." And then we should try to indicate the degree of safety or risk. So . . .

2. **Put numbers on risks if possible.** Don't just say the risk is small or great. Is the risk 1 in 100, or 1,000, or 1 million, or what?

3. **Put a "per unit of time" on the risks.** If the risk is 1 in 1,000, is that for a day, a month, a year, or a lifetime?

4. **Personalize the risk numbers.** In addition to saying "the U.S. homicide rate is 8.0 per 100,000 per year," you can say "one person in every 12,500 will

be a homicide victim this year, if current rates continue."

5. Include the uncertainties. Once more: If the studies are weak, say so. If no one knows, say so. Don't hesitate to say "might," or "is believed to," or just "some experts believe." Use other qualifiers when appropriate.

6. Use ranges, rather than just worst-case figures. Avoid: "As many as a jillion could be killed." Include the worst-case number only as part of a range that includes both low and high estimates.

7. Put a human feel on the figures when you can. Jim Detjen, who was a top reporter for the *Philadelphia Inquirer,* says: "Write about things in a way your readers can relate to. Don't just say so many parts per million of sulfur dioxide are going into the air; explain how those levels can trigger asthmatic attacks among the sick and elderly."

8. Put a human face on the story when appropriate. Detjen again: "Find and write about environmental victims. But don't be irresponsible. You don't need to sensationalize. An accurate picture is often alarming enough."[12]

9. Compare risks. How does an environmental or other risk compare to the chance of being killed in a traffic accident? Or to some other event that people can relate to?

At this writing, the risk of dying in a motor vehicle accident in the United States is 1 in 6,500 per year.

You also can compare a risk to the chance of being struck by lightning—but use care in doing so. Lightning is a serious problem that annually kills about 90 Americans—that is, 1 in every 3 million. So a comparable national environmental or other risk would kill as many people as might die in the crash of a medium-sized airliner.

Lightning also provides a reminder that risk is often individualized. If you're a golfer who doesn't heed warnings to seek safety during a thunderstorm, your risks go way up.

Caution: Someone can make any risk seem relatively small by comparing it to cigarette smoking, which kills about 400,000 Americans a year. Something can kill many, many fewer people and still rank as a major catastrophe.

10. Don't forget denominators. If you report an illness has struck 100 people in some town, you should report 100 out of how many.

11. Recognize that people choose to accept some risks. Let Douglas Hofstadter stir your thinking: "Can you imagine how we would react if someone said . . . 'Hey, everybody! I've come up with a really nifty invention. Unfortunately it has a minor defect. Every [18 years or so], it will wipe out about as many Americans as the population of San Francisco!' That's what automobile accidents do."[13]

But who wants to go back to the horse and buggy? Also remember: It's not illogical for us to accept some risks associated with things that we choose to do, while opposing other risks that are imposed upon us.

12. Help people cut their risk when you can. *Examples:* When writing or talking about high levels of radon gas in some homes, tell the homeowners what they can do to reduce the levels of this naturally occurring gas. Tell them how pipes, fans, and other methods can be used to make their homes safer.[14]

When appropriate, tell about recycling, or ways to cut back on garden chemicals, or other steps that may be helpful. When appropriate, tell readers about the safe installation of children's car seats, or where to get this information.[15]

When writing about all sorts of environmental or other risk-reduction subjects, when possible give your readers or viewers a source or a web site where they can get more information. But be confident of the source, check out the site first, and make sure the information is worth passing on.

13. Ask questions about the proposed solutions too.

Sometimes the proposed fix creates a new problem, maybe even worse than the original problem.

Example: In the 1990 Clean Air Act, Congress required that areas of the county with ozone smog problems use "reformulated gasoline," with increased oxygen content. Urban areas in 17 states had acted by 2000, most of them by using the oxygen additive methyl tertiary-butyl ether (MTBE). While this additive prevents smog, it is very soluble in water and does not "cling" to soil well. It has turned out to be a major cause of groundwater contamination.

"We need to begin now to eliminate MTBE from gasoline and move to *safer* alternatives, like ethanol," said Carol Browner, administrator of the federal Environment Protection Agency.[16] We're glad she used the word "safer" (we added the italics) rather than "safe," in keeping with the first tip on this list.

14. Avoid scaring people out of ignorance. Says John Ullmann, the first executive director of Investigative Reporters and Editors and now executive director of Macalester College's World Press Institute: "Often we're talking about stories that can scare people to death, if we don't do them well. I mean sometimes we are a walking time-bomb ourselves, because we're so ignorant."[17] So . . .

15. Read. Learn. Cultivate long-term sources, such as physicians, physicists, chemists, biologists, engineers, informed officials, and other experts in fields dealing with various reporting areas. These people will be far easier to tap, and far more forthcoming, once they know you've done some homework.

16. Don't be afraid to challenge an expert. Dr. Dorothy Nelkin at Cornell University says, "The most serious problem" in reporting on risk may be the reluctance of some journalists to challenge their sources and "those who use the authority of science to shape the public view." Maintain "the spirit of independent, critical inquiry that has guided good investigation in other areas."[18]

17. Broaden your concept of good sources. Sometimes the people "who really know what's going on" aren't the conventional experts, Detjen pointed out. On pollution, you may want to talk with fishermen, foresters, or airline pilots.[19] For an article on road rage or other traffic risks, we suggest talking to cab drivers, who see it all every day and night.

18. "Follow up, follow up, follow up," Detjen adds. Environmental problems don't go away. Is substance X still a problem? What, if anything, has been done a few years down the road? We would add that the "one-shot exposé," without sustained follow-up, is a common news media sin. It does little good to expose a problem about anything unless you stay with it. Follow up the administrative, legislative, industry, or community action. Report what, if anything, gets done.

More about risks—For information on **risk ratios**, see "Putting Numbers on Risks" in Chapter 7. For cautions in reporting **lifetime risks** (such as women's one-in-nine risk of breast cancer), see "'Lifetime Risk' and 'Cancer Clusters'" also in Chapter 7. For examples of people's **varying views about risks**, see "Entertainment: Risk to Whom?" in Chapter 11.

Polls: Measuring What We Think 10

A president cannot always be popular.

—Harry Truman

Statistics are the heart of democracy.

—Simeon Strunsky

When you come to a fork in the road, take it.

—Yogi Berra

————— & & & —————

We breathlessly await, and often are influenced by, the results of political polls and other polling that try to tell us what we are thinking. But keep in mind how lack of care can skew a poll's findings.

Ross Perot, founder of the Reform Party, asked in a mail-in poll: "Should laws be passed to eliminate all possibilities of special interests giving huge sums of money to candidates?" Ninety-nine percent of the people who responded said yes.

Then the prestigious polling firm Yankelovich and Partners asked the very same question to a scientifically based, national sampling of Americans. Now 80 percent said yes.

Finally the polling firm asked a more neutral version of the question, to another scientifically based sampling of people across the nation: "Should laws be passed to prohibit interest groups from contributing to campaigns, or do groups have a right to contribute to the candidate they support?" Those in favor of prohibiting contributions dropped to 40 percent.[1]

Perot's poll violated two basic tenets of scientific polling. First, it was published in a magazine and was dependent on which readers chose to mail in their answers. Thus the people polled were self-selected and not a random sampling of voters. Second, Perot's question was biased—perhaps unintentionally, out of his political zeal.

Polling with Care

There are four basic things for journalists and poll-followers to keep in mind:

1. Random sampling can make 1 = 200,000. In a typical national poll, about 1,000 people may be interviewed to get results showing what 200 million American adults think about political candidates or issues. That means that the poll is using the response of each person interviewed to represent what 200,000 people think. The principle is the same for a state or regional poll, although the numbers will vary.

To make all this work, the selection of people polled must be random. That's the only way they can be considered representative of all Americans (or all members of whatever population is being polled).

You can't use the first 1,000 people that pass you on the street. You can't use a typical TV show "poll"— the people watching the show and phoning in are self-selected. You can't depend on who does or doesn't decide to mail back a magazine questionnaire, as Perot did.

Typically, pollsters use a random selection of phone numbers to select the people they interview. The pollsters then can make adjustments, if necessary, to make sure the sampling is representative of the desired population. For example, here's how the Minnesota Poll in the *Star Tribune* of Minneapolis–St. Paul explains this part of its polling technique to its readers:

"A random-digit-dial telephone sample of 1,001 adult Minnesotans" was used. "Results for the poll were weighted for age, gender and education to make sure that the sample reflected . . . census estimates for Minnesota's adult population."[2]

2. The size of a poll determines its margin of sampling error. The more people polled, the smaller the margin of sampling error. A *New York Times* poll used admirable candor to tell readers about a poll with 900 adults:

"In theory, in 19 cases out of 20, the results based on such samples will differ by no more than 3 percentage points in either direction from that which would have been obtained by interviewing all adult New Yorkers. For smaller groups, the potential error is greater. For all whites, plus or minus 4 percentage points. For all blacks, it is plus or minus 7 points.

"In addition to sampling error, the practical difficulties of conducting any survey of public opinion may introduce other sources of error into the poll."[3]

When it's too close to call, a poll should admit it. If candidate A is leading candidate B but the poll's results are still within its margin of sampling error, the news report should clearly say so. The same applies to polls that probe issues or attitudes.

The Minnesota Poll uses language that, after making points similar to the *New York Times*'s explanation to its readers, ends by saying: "Other things affect results, such as question wording and the changes of opinion over time."[4] That leads us to . . .

3. Good questions are vital to avoid tilting responses. The questions asked are crucial to a poll's validity, as the Perot poll example at the start of this chapter shows. The Pew Research Center for the People and the Press came up with another innovative test. In a special poll, the Pew Research Center first noted that President Clinton had proposed setting aside about two-thirds of an expected budget surplus to fix the Social Security system. The Pew Center poll then . . .

• Asked some people: Should the rest of the budget surplus be used for a tax cut, or should this money "be used to fund new government programs." The results: 60 percent said cut taxes, and only 25 percent said fund new programs. Eleven percent said the money should be used for other purposes.

• Asked another group of people: Should the rest of the surplus be used for a tax cut or for spending "for education, the environment, health care, crime-fighting and military defense." Now only 22 percent said cut taxes, and 69 percent said spend it on the listed programs. Six percent said use the money for other purposes.

(The figures don't add up to 100 percent because some people polled said they didn't know, or they didn't want to answer.)[5]

The order in which questions are asked also may affect the results. If you first ask pointed questions about problems that one candidate is having, you may skew the results of a following how-will-you-vote question.

A *related example:* In a poll at the height of the Cold War in the 1950s, Americans were asked if they thought that the United States should allow "Communist reporters from other countries [to] come in here and send back to their papers the news as they see it." Only 36 percent said yes. But the yes answers increased to 73 percent when the very same question was preceded by one asking if Russia should admit American reporters.[6]

4. A poll is only a snapshot, taken at one point in time. At best, polls can only tell what people are thinking when they are polled. So put polls to these tests:

• Could the timing of the poll skew the results? If a poll is taken before a candidate made a serious gaffe but the poll is not published until afterward, that should be clearly noted. If a poll on gun possession was taken before the Columbine shootings but published a few days after the shootings, the reader certainly should be informed.

• Is one candidate likely to get more of his or her supporters to the polls on election day? As elections near, polltakers ask questions designed to weed out participants who are unlikely to vote on election day. (*Examples:* Are you registered? Did you vote in the last election? How interested are you in this election?)[7] Reporters should report, where appropriate, when a particular candidate's appeal might bring out more voters on election day.

Of course, nothing can guarantee that any specific poll will be on target. Pollster Burns W. Roper was once asked the same question that his firm had asked in a poll: How do you assess the accuracy of polls? His response: "Usually accurate."[8]

Case Histories: Ventura, Reagan, and Bush

Ventura's victory and who wasn't surprised—Here's an example of how a poll can be right even when it doesn't call the winner:

When ex-pro-wrestler Jesse ("the Body") Ventura was elected Minnesota governor in 1998, readers of the *Star Tribune* in Minneapolis–St. Paul clearly weren't as surprised as most Americans. Two days earlier, the newspaper's Minnesota Poll was able to tell its readers that while Ventura was still running number three in the three-man race, each contender "has a real chance of claiming the governor's office on election day."

Eight percentage points divided the three candidates, which was more than the margin of sampling error. But the newspaper cited the poll's trend data to show how Ventura was gaining ground in an unusually volatile race. The poll data also showed that many Minnesotans felt Ventura was in tune with them on key issues, indicating that he might get some late-minute converts.

And the poll article said the winner could be determined by which candidate could do the best job of getting his voters to the polls. That's just what Ventura did to win.[9]

Reagan and the ABCs of polling—Within a few weeks in July 1984, five major polls gave President Reagan a lead varying from 1 to 26 points over Walter Mondale. Who was near the mark at that point? We have no idea. But in their final, most careful predictions on election eve, seven polls gave the president leads that varied from 10 to 25 points. He won by 18 points.

The veteran Louis Harris, off 6 points, said he had chosen to rely on his last day of polling instead of the last three days, which had generally proved more accurate in the past.[10] At best, says pollster Richard Wirthlin, polling is an "ABC science, Almost Being Certain," because "we are not dealing with reality directly, but through a mirror darkly clouded."[11]

Reporting the Bush-Gore count—and eating some crow—The pre-election polls showed some volatile ups and downs for George W. Bush and Al Gore during their long campaign for president in 2000. But during the last days before the election, the major national polls narrowed sharply. Bush tended to have a slight lead. But the candidates were within a few percentage points of each other—within the polls' margins of sampling error.

"It turned out that almost everyone [conducting polls] produced a result that this was going to be a close election and a very long [election] night," said Kathleen Frankovic, director of surveys at CBS. It's just that nobody could have predicted how close. Or how l-o-n-g.[12]

Throughout election night, the TV networks reported that Gore's and Bush's nationwide totals were very close in popular votes, and in the electoral votes that would determine the winner.

The TV maps used red and blue to show which candidate had "won" individual states. The trouble was, the color for electoral-vote-rich Florida kept changing.

Early in the evening, the networks projected that Florida had gone for Gore. Whoops! Within two hours the networks retracted that, saying that state was too close to call. "Oh waiter—one order of crow," Jeff Greenfield, the CNN analyst, told his network's audience.

Reason for this about-face: Problems had become apparent in data supplied by Voter News Service, a media consortium. The news service did exit-polling—by asking a random sampling of people leaving selected voting places how they had cast their ballots—and also collected actual voting returns. A clerical input error had distorted one county's data for awhile, and some of the exit polling results had overstated Gore's advantage.

After midnight, the networks reported that Florida now had gone for *Bush* rather than Gore, pushing Bush over the top in nationwide electoral votes. The networks (and some newspapers) declared Bush president-elect. Whoops again! Within about an hour they admitted that they had goofed. The Florida race—and therefore the national electoral vote totals—was *again* classified as too close to call.

Reason for about-face number two: Al Ortiz, executive producer of CBS's coverage, said the network had thought Bush's lead in Florida was too large for Gore to overcome. "It looked like a solid margin that was going to hold," he said. But then it become apparent that Voter News Service had underestimated how many votes were yet to be counted.

It wasn't until 36 days later that the final word was in. After rancorous recounts and controversial court rulings, Gore conceded that he had lost Florida by a razor-thin margin. Bush was president-elect.

Two key lessons from election night: Polls aren't the only potential problem area for election numbers. Watch 'em all. And in the journalistic race to call the winner, don't let competitive juices cloud clear thinking.

Other Poll-Watching Advice

Various experts make these points:

Know when to say or write "percentage points" rather than "percent." Rob Daves, director of the Minnesota Poll at the *Star Tribune,* offers these guidelines to make things clear, correct, and consistent:

- Use "percentage points" when you are talking about the differences between percents. For example, if 60 percent of the poll's participants favor can-

didate A and 40 percent favor candidate B, write it, "Candidate A has a 20 *percentage point* lead over B in the poll."
• Use "percentage points" when you are expressing a margin of sampling error. *Example:* "The poll's margin of sampling error is plus or minus 3 *percentage points.*"[13]

Don't magnify a small change from one poll to the next. If the president's approval rating goes from 59 to 58 percent, or one candidate's standing edges up 2 points, it's worth mentioning. But only if the trend continues is it worth putting in the bank.

Put extra confidence in findings when more than one poll—asking approximately the same questions agree.

Watch the who, why, and when of special-interest polling. Some polls are sponsored by companies or advocacy groups yet are conducted by reputable polling organizations. Some polls also are conducted for political candidates or parties. This doesn't mean the results can't be valid. But readers and viewers should be told enough to ask themselves: Why was this poll taken? Or taken at this time? Always: Were the questions fair?

Watch out for political "push polling." Here's how this pseudo-polling, political telemarketing technique is done:

The telephone caller uses the pretext of taking a poll, but the real purpose is to "sell"—or push—a particular political candidate. The caller does this by presenting false or misleading information about the candidate's opponent, then asking how this will affect voter preference.

The American Association for Public Opinion Research warns that push polling "can easily be confused with real polls," which in turn can "damage the reputation of legitimate polling" and discourage people from participating in proper polls.

Watch out for how others use polls. To quote Robert
Samuelson, *Newsweek* economics columnist:
"To prove the popularity of [an administration's] tax
plan, you cite surveys showing that roughly half of the
public favor it, with about a third against. To demonstrate
opposition, you cite polls indicating large majorities
against specific proposals, such as the elimination of the
deduction for local taxes. In fact, inconsistent results
often indicate just that: The public is ambivalent."[14]

Let polling help you tell other types of stories. The
value of polls goes beyond political races and hot-button
issues. One of the authors of this book (Cope) used
polling as a major part of a five-part series on preventive
health care in the *Star Tribune* of Minneapolis–St. Paul. He
was able to start one article in the series, "Most
Minnesotans buckle up for safety—then speed." And
another article: "Minnesotans are smoking less, but being
bothered by other people's smoke more."[15]

Know where to get more information. The Minnesota
Poll's Daves recommends two Internet sites:

• The web site of the National Council on Public
Polls is *www.ncpp.org*. You can read "20 questions a
journalist should ask about poll results" and get
other information as well.
• The web site for the American Association for
Public Opinion Research, with information about
"push polling" and other topics, is www.aapor.org.

Another Case History: Asking about Sex

The subject of sex shows that there are pollsters and
pollsters. In 1987, author and social investigator Shere
Hite published her third book on men and women in bed

and out. Hite's findings—on women's attitudes about men, sex, and personal and marital relationships—put her on the cover of *Time* and launched a flood of news stories and TV talk.

Hite had distributed 100,000 detailed questionnaires, seeking answers to 127 questions, to women in groups of many kinds all over the country. She received only 4,500 replies. On the basis of those, she reported that 84 percent of the women in her study were dissatisfied with their marital or other intimate relationships. She reported that 78 percent said that they were generally not treated as equals by men and that 70 percent of those married more than five years had had affairs. And so on, with a number of answers and Hite's elaborations indicating that women in general are mainly unhappy with their relationships.

Women in general? Hite said at one point in her book that "no one can generalize" from her findings. Yet she also claimed that her 4,500 respondents were typical of all American women and that her results could be replicated on a much larger scale without a huge difference in results.

Critics—virtually all social scientists and students of public opinion who commented—said her sample was almost certainly heavily weighted with the unhappiest women, those who took the time to answer the lengthy questionnaire. The critics did not doubt that many women feel the same way as Hite's respondents. They just did not know how many.

Testing Hite's findings, a *Washington Post*-ABC News polling team questioned a representative sample—representative by usual polling methods—of 767 women and 738 men across the nation. That poll found that 93 percent of the married and single women said they were satisfied with their relationships, 81 percent said they were treated as equals most of the time, and only 7 percent reported affairs.

That survey, like most surveys, was conducted by phone. Hite said women would not be candid to a telephone caller. Jeff Alderman, ABC polling director, replied, "Over the phone, people will say things to us they wouldn't say to a neighbor. We've never had any indication they lie." But Richard Morin, *Washington Post* polling director, conceded that these sunny results should be interpreted with some care too, since "telephone surveys like this might be expected to overstate satisfaction with personal relationships, and understate, to a significantly greater degree, the extent of socially unacceptable behavior such as adultery."[16]

Who was closer to the truth? We don't know, but we do know that telephone surveys of small, well-selected samples can at least come within hail of the truth when they are tested in elections. Hite, in contrast, was no scientific sampler of public opinion. She nonetheless uncovered hundreds of revealing stories and strong emotions. We deserve a look as deep and searching as hers at male-female relationships. But, so important is the subject, we deserve a study with results as valid as the most careful political poll.

Potential Perils of "Snowball Samples"

Reporters occasionally borrow a page from polling, without claiming to have a scientifically accurate poll. They interview a dozen, maybe many more, supposedly randomly chosen people in a community to get a general feeling of attitudes about an election, about an issue, or about a controversy. An experienced editor cautions:

They'll make this common mistake: They'll ask somebody— somebody picked at random, perhaps—a question, but then take *that* person's recommendation on the next person to talk to, because the first person has said, 'I'll tell you somebody else who knows a lot about that.'

At that point they no longer have a random sample. I think the expression for this is a *snowball sample*. What made me aware of it was a survey we had a couple of professors do, a survey of Vietnamese refugees in this country, about their treatment in refugee camps back in Vietnam. [The professors] interviewed one family, then that family knew another family, and so on. They soon realized they were getting only one story and changed their methodology. It makes you realize how easily you can skew things.[17]

A statistician adds: True enough and worth guarding against, but snowball sampling can be a good way to collect information about a particular class of persons with the same interests or problems. Just don't confuse them with a representative sample of a broader population.

What Focus Groups Can and Can't Do

Political candidates and business firms also use *focus groups* to gauge public opinion. Typically, a small group of people is brought together for an in-depth interview by a trained moderator. The moderator uses follow-up questions to probe deeper than a poll would allow. And since it's done in person rather than over the phone, the people being interviewed can be shown a company's new product or a planned TV ad.

This approach may uncover a surprise finding that a pollster would not have thought to ask about. A good focus group moderator is much like a good reporter conducting a group interview.

But focus groups aren't scientific polls. Their findings must be viewed with caution. The groups are too small to serve as a representative sampling of the public. There's no way to know how widespread the group's opinions apply. And when a reporter is told that a political party's or a company's focus group has found something that favors candidate X or company Y, the reporter can't readily tell whether the focus group discussion was tilted in some way.

Checklist—See "Checklists for Studies and Polls" in the Appendix for a quick-reference checklist of this chapter's four polling basics.

Politics, Your Pocketbook, and Plenty More

Democracy is the worst form of government, except all those other forms that have been tried from time to time.

—Sir Winston Churchill

Sound policies rest on good information.

—Dr. Frederick Mosteller

——— *& & &* ———

Government officials and others are continually telling us "we have learned that . . ." or "statistics show that . . ." or "the computer shows. . . ." This is followed by words that depend on numbers.

There is every reason to apply some good-sense tests to all such statements by politicians, government officials, economists, salespersons, sports coaches, and others. We must identify the good and thwart any attempts to pull statistics over our eyes.

For starters, we can use many of the tests that have been discussed earlier in the book. We can ask questions such as: How do you know? What numbers lead you to your conclusion? What studies or other methods were used to gather the numbers? How valid, how reliable, how probable are they? Could bias affect the figures—or the conclusions being drawn from them?

And there are specific things to be alert to in various fields.

In a moment we'll tell you about the Lake Wobegon Effect, which tends to make all schools look good. We'll look at some surprising crime statistics and some advertising hoodwinks. We'll look at other numbers in fields, ranging from travel to the weather and from world affairs to the slumps and dunks of the sports world. We'll even revisit the O.J. Simpson trial.

But first, let's focus on some things that can interfere with our clear thinking.

Statistical Shenanigans

Statistician Nancy Lyon Spruill, writing in the *Washington Post,* warned against several types of statistical shenanigans. She and others describe them as politicians' tricks—but they are by no means confined to politicians:[1]

1. **The everything-is-going-up statistic.** More people are employed, or more people are getting support payments, or whatever. Correct, because there are more people than ever. A more informative statistic would be the employment or unemployment *rate* or the portion of the population getting welfare payments.

Another example: An Agriculture Department official once hailed the finding that pork exports had tripled in a two-month period. Further analysis, by others, showed that few pork products were then being exported. Anytime "you start . . . with a small base, the percentage increase is going to be large."[2]

2. **The best-foot statistic.** Selecting whatever number best supports a case, as in choosing between median and mean family income. If the rich get richer and the poor get poorer, the median might

stay unchanged. If a few get richer, the mean income will be dragged up, even if incomes for most families remain unchanged.

Another example: Picking the best-sounding year (or years) for comparison. To show an increase in family income, you can compare the prosperous present with a recession year.

3. The gee-whiz or half-truth statistic. *Example:* using numbers for only part of the population. If the unemployment rate doesn't say what you want, talk about the rate for teenagers or the rate in industrial states.

Another example: To deplore defense spending, tell how increases in defense spending have increased the national debt; don't mention how increases in domestic spending have done the same thing.

4. The everyone-is-average statistic. We're told that women can't be combat soldiers because the average man can lift more weight than the average woman. But many women can and do lift more weight than many men.

5. The coincidence statistic. Whoever is in office is blamed for a recession, though economists can't agree on the cause. Whoever is in office takes credit for a boom, though ditto.

6. The meaningless statistic. A sixth mischievous statistic is from *Fortune* writer Daniel Seligman, in an article titled, "We're Drowning in Phony Statistics":[3] A New York City mayor once said that the "overall cleanliness of the streets has risen to 85 percent," up from 56 percent five years earlier. By what objective criteria? Neither the mayor nor his aides could cite any (although it might have been possible to develop some).

The antidotes for these offenses:

- **Ask for *all* the numbers,** then see if they are appropriate ones for drawing any conclusions.
- **Calculate your own rates of change** from what seem to be sensible bases.
- **Look at changes over several years,** not just a short time.
- **Keep asking, "How do you know?"**

Newsy Numbers on Numerous Fronts

Now a look at examples of newsy numbers on numerous fronts (with some broader take-home messages in **boldface**):

Education: The Lake Wobegon Effect

It's a result that any high-school math student would question: Studies show that most school districts across the nation report that their students score above the national average on standardized tests, the *New York Times* reported.

How could so many schools beat the average? Cheating has been reported in a few schools. More often, school officials may switch from one form of test to another to get the good scores they crave, the 1999 *New York Times* article said.[4]

The results have been nicknamed the Lake Wobegon Effect. The reference is to author Garrison Keillor's fictional Minnesota community, where the women are strong, the men good-looking, and the children are all above average.

The better something sounds, the deeper you may need to probe.

Crime: Where You Draw the Line

Washington, D.C., was dubbed the nation's "murder capital" in the late 1980s, based on statistics from cities across the nation. Malcolm Gladwell, a *Washington Post* financial reporter, used his numbers-sense to show that the label was undeserved. Washington's problem, he found, had more to do with the historical accident that produced that city's political boundaries.[5]

Many other cities encompass relatively large—and relatively safe—suburban fringes. Washington, D.C., is not part of any state and has never been able to annex suburban areas that could dilute the city's crime statistics. If Washington's borders took in "35 percent of the surrounding metro population, as Philadelphia's borders do, the city's murder rate would drop out of the top 10," Gladwell showed.

Another factor helps other cities. "Many cities have pockets of crime just outside their boundaries," Gladwell noted. For example, Compton, California, which has had a high murder rate, lies just outside the Los Angeles city line; Compton's murders don't affect the Los Angeles murder rate.

This isn't just a crime phenomenon. It distorts the Washington, D.C., infant mortality rate too, Gladwell discovered. And a lot of other things, no doubt.

Compare cities with care.

More about crime in "Putting Statistics to Good Use" later in this chapter.

Courts: Lessons from the O.J. Simpson Trial

The O.J. Simpson trial made DNA analysis a household phrase. It also might make the job of statisticians and reporters a bit easier as they try to tell the public what they know or don't know. The trial, with its "not guilty" verdict, whatever its other merits or demerits, was an unprecedented lesson in:

- The inevitability of uncertainty. The fact that the gathering of evidence, by a scientist or policeman, is seldom perfect.
- The fact that we must nonetheless try to draw conclusions, and often act, on the best evidence at hand.
- The nature of probability, in this case the probability that a match of DNA (the chemical basis of all our genes) says this person is it. And the fact that we must often rely on probabilities.[6]

DNA: From History to Today's Bedside

The political opponents of Thomas Jefferson, the nation's third president, leveled a charge in 1802 that reverberates to this day. They alleged that Jefferson had fathered a son of one of his slaves, Sally Hemings. Historical speculation simmered for almost two centuries before coming to a boil.

Jefferson is no longer around today to give a blood sample, which limits the type of DNA testing that can be done to see whether there is a paternity link. But some enterprising scientists did the next best thing. They tested blood from descendants of Jefferson's paternal grandfather and compared it with blood from Hemings's descendants. The Jefferson and the Hemings descendants both had a male-line DNA marker that would normally be found in less than 1 percent of all men.

"The simplest and most probable explanations for our molecular [DNA] findings are that Thomas Jefferson . . . was the father of Eston [Hemings]," the researchers reported in the journal *Nature* in 1998. Then they added: "We cannot completely rule out other explanations of our findings based on illegitimacy in various lines of descent." For example: A male relative of Jefferson might have introduced the genetic marker into the Hemings family tree. But there is no historical evidence to support such conjecture, the researchers added.

Many news publications weren't as cautious as the researchers. The word "proof" was used too often, although some publications did use careful terms like "found evidence" or "suggests." The Statistical Assessment Service, a watchdog group that tracks news reports, noted that one newspaper went so far as to headline the story: "Adulterer on Mt. Rushmore."[7]

Just to make the scientific caution crystal clear: The head of the research team wrote a letter, published in the *New York Times*, saying again, "This study could not prove anything conclusively."

Just to make the practical point clear: The Thomas Jefferson Memorial Foundation said in early 2000 that, based on both the scientific and the historical evidence, it now accepts the "strong likelihood" that Jefferson fathered at least one Hemings child.[8]

Proper qualifications don't weaken a story; they add credibility.

As we enter the 21st century, you can be sure that DNA will continue in the news in another very important way. Researchers are working to find how to use DNA to treat various diseases. This gene-therapy frontier could be revolutionary. But it must meet the tough statistical tests of science to prove it can help ill patients. And other questions remain, such as the risk of serious side effects.

Sports: Slumps, Dunks, and More

"The species *homo sapiens* has a powerful propensity to believe that one can find a pattern even when there is no pattern to be found," when random variability or chance produces what only seems to be a pattern. So writes Dr. Julian L. Simon, an economist at the University of Maryland.[9]

Take baseball, he says. A generally good hitter strikes out three or four consecutive times at bat. The coach then declares a "slump" and pulls him out of the lineup. But studies show that short-term performance in most sports varies in the same way that a run of random numbers of coin flips varies. Similarly, it's been shown that a basketball player's chance of making a basket on each try is unaffected by whether he made or missed the previous shot.

There are indeed long-term trends in sports. A good player can become a poor or aging one. But beware of short-term predictions—in sports, economics, and other fields. As one statistician put it, "Even though there may be real trends in a system, many systems inherently have a very large random component which over short terms may obscure the long-term trends."[10]

Reporters love predictions. Sometimes too much.

On the road to the National Football League's 2000 Super Bowl: Some teams in the first week of playoffs got a "bye"—a week off without a game. And some TV sports commentators made a big deal out of the fact that most of these teams won their games in the following week, concluding that these teams had benefited from a week of rest and extra planning. The unstated bias: The teams that got the byes had earned them, by having the best statistical won-lost records in the regular season. These teams simply continued their winning ways the next week.

A reminder: Always look for other possible explanations.

Your Pocketbook: Ads and Stocks

Robert Hooke, the statistician and author, warns us about ads that say: "Independent laboratory tests show that no other leading product is more effective than ours." His translation: "A [purposely] small test was run among the leading products, and no significant difference was observed among the products tested. . . . There are people around who can make good news for themselves out of anything."[11]

Darrell Huff, author of the small 1954 book "How to Lie with Statistics," adds this advertising shenanigan:[12]

"If you can't prove what you want to prove, demonstrate something else and pretend that they are the same thing. . . . You can't prove that your nostrum cures colds, but you can publish a sworn laboratory report that half an ounce of the stuff killed 31,108 germs in a test tube. . . . It is not up to you . . . to point out that an antiseptic that works well in a test tube may not perform in the human throat. . . . [And] don't confuse the issue by telling what kind of germ you killed."

Huff also tells of a juice extractor that was widely advertised as one that "extracts 26 percent more juice." More than what? Inquiry showed "only that this juicer got that much more juice than an old-fashioned hand-reamer," though it still might be the poorest electrical juicer on the market.

It could be "twice as many accidents," or "twice as toxic." It means nothing unless you answer: More than what?

Psst! I've got a hot stock tip I'll sell you . . .

Watch out, warns Dr. Simon at the University of Maryland. A stock-picker's great record may be more luck than skill. Statistics tell us that some people, by chance alone, will pick a portfolio that will go up, just as a few people among many flip several heads in a row.

Here's how hard it is to beat the market: You can assume that the nation's dozen largest stock mutual funds have some of the world's best money-managers running them. One of the 12 is an index fund that simply tracks the 500 stocks in the Standard and Poor's 500, representing most of the nation's largest companies. Of the other 11 actively managed funds, only 3 beat the Standard and Poor's 500 when results over five years (1996 through 2000) are considered.[13]

More about Money: The Stop-Smoking Paradox

Conventional wisdom long assumed that cigarette smoking costs society millions or billions of dollars, by increasing the risk of heart disease, cancer, and other expensive-to-treat illnesses. A 1997 study by Dutch researchers, reported in the *New England Journal of Medicine,* concluded otherwise. Smoking may actually save society money in the long run, because smokers don't live as long as other folks. They often die of smoking-related diseases before reaching the age where chronic illnesses give a big push to health costs.

But don't jump to the conclusion that the Dutch researchers think smokers should continue to puff away.

"We believe that in formulating public health policy, whether or not smokers impose a net financial burden ought to be of very limited importance," they said. The important thing is that smoking takes an unacceptable heavy toll in death, disease, and their effects on families. "The objective of a policy on smoking should be simple and clear: Smoking should be discouraged."[14]

Some other types of prevention efforts, such as screening for cholesterol levels to start early treatment, also don't save money, other studies suggest. But they can save many lives. And they can avoid a lot of pain, expense, and other problems.[15]

Question all money-making and money-savings claims.

Wealth, Welfare, and Biz Taxes: Mixed Pictures

As the United States entered the 21st century, it had the lowest unemployment rate in 30 years. And a Federal Reserve report showed that the typical American family's net worth increased 18 percent from 1995 to 1998, the latest year for which data were available. (Typical was defined as the median, where half the families have larger net worths and half have smaller ones.)

But when you probe deeper into the Fed report, you find:

- Average incomes have risen only modestly. It's the rising stock and mutual-fund holdings by many middle- and upper-income families, propelled by a soaring bull market, that have fueled the big increases in net worth.
- Yes, welfare rolls are down. But the distribution of wealth has been far from even. The net worth of fam-

ilies with incomes of less than $25,000, which had
been rising in the early 1990s, decreased between
1995 and 1998. The poverty rate has declined, but
not as much as in previous economic expansions.[16]

**A reminder: You often must break figures down to
get the full picture.**
Corporate profits have been growing even faster than
family incomes. But a revealing *New York Times* report
pointed out that taxes paid by companies to the Internal
Revenue Service have fallen. Key reasons: Legal tax credits and deductions for stock options for employees reduce
many companies' taxes. And the growing use of tax shel-
ters, some of which the government is questioning, helps
some firms.[17]

Shopping: Are Retail Sales Really That Good?

Author Huff urges us to consider: "What's missing?"
A business story says that April retail sales are well
ahead of April's the year before. Left unstated: the fact
that Easter came in March the first year and in April the
second.
**"What's missing?" is another way of saying: Look for
other possible explanations.**

Transportation: Drive or Fly?

In the wake of the 1999 crash of EgyptAir Flight 990,
with the loss of 217 lives, the *New York Times* reminded us
that airline travel is, overall, statistically safer than driving
your car. If air-crash stories induced just 1 percent of
domestic travelers to switch from planes to cars over the

next year, the article calculated that could result in 40 additional deaths.

The article draws support for this line of reasoning from Barry Glassner, a professor of sociology at the University of Southern California: "What the public needs after an airplane crash is reassurance about the safety of air travel. Instead, the media provide a laundry list of past crashes and possible dangers."[18]

People just feel safer in their cars, which they can (or think they can) control.

Statistics can provide a provocative bonus to a big news story.

World Affairs: Confusing Counts

Professor I. Richard Savage at Yale University notes that news of the Vietnam War "gave ample suggestion that statistics was being used for self-deception." He quotes then Defense Secretary Robert McNamara: "You couldn't reconcile the number of the enemy, the level of infiltration, the body count, and the resulting figures. It just didn't add up. I never did get . . . a balanced equation."[19] Nor did perceptive reporters.

Lobbying: The Flip Side Can Be True Too

During a 1990 debate over provisions in the Clean Air Act, a law was proposed to remove more auto-tailpipe emissions. The old law called for a 96 percent reduction in emissions. The new law would have increased the 96 percent to 98 percent.

The auto industry called it an expensive and meaningless 2 percentage point increase in removal. Environmentalists said it would result in a 50 percent decrease in the remaining automobile pollution.[20]

Both viewpoints pass math muster, so report both.
But don't stop there. Tell what's known, and what's
unknown, about what this change would mean to your
readers or viewers.

Worker Safety: Hidden Numbers

A page-one article in the *New York Times* told us that
"workers at New York City building sites have the highest
rate of death from unsafe conditions among the nation's
35 largest cities."[21]

How many workers have been dying? We had to read
to the 14th paragraph, on the jump page inside the second section, to learn that from 1979 through 1985 the
numbers of deaths varied from 7 to 15 a year. We had to
get to the 25th paragraph to find the *rate* described in the
first paragraph: 7.61 deaths for each billion dollars of construction, much higher than the average 3.3 deaths in the
35 cities.

Why couldn't the story have told us right at the out-
set: "Between 7 and 15 New York City workers a year die in
construction accidents"? Fear of numbers? Fear that even
New York Times readers fear numbers? Fear that 7 to 15
deaths a year wouldn't sound impressive in the big, violent
city? We don't know.

Don't bury the numbers if the numbers are the story.

Entertainment: Risk to Whom?

This tale may just be a tale, but it's a fun one that a
Harvard biologist (in a letter appearing in the journal
Science) used to make a point about viewing things from
different perspectives:

Back in 1974, Evel Knievel was about to attempt to jump over the Snake River Canyon in a rocket car. The car's designer told a TV reporter that Knievel had about an 80 percent chance of success.

"That good?" replied the TV reporter, apparently coming into the interview fearing the worst.

"Good?" shot back the designer. "You think that's *good?*"

We don't know what Knievel thought of his chances. Was he successful? It depends on how you define success. His rocket car didn't make it across. But an emergency parachute did open to save Knievel's life.

Remember: Risk perception varies from one person to another.

Weather: Bedroom and Other Behavior

We regularly read about weather records—the hottest day, coldest day, or whatever in so-many years. One of this book's coauthors (Cope) went to other statistics to tell readers of the *Star Tribune* in Minneapolis–St. Paul how the weather really affects their everyday lives.

Do Minnesota's long, cold nights in December and January bring bedroom behavior that results in an increased birth rate nine months later? No. March is the leading month for births in Minnesota. Count back the gestational nine months and you're at June—the month with the shortest nights in the year.

Do traffic fatalities rise in Minnesota during the ice and snow season? No. Total accidents increase. But that's primarily because of fender-benders. Higher speeds in the summer, along with more travel then, explain the higher death toll.

Does it get too cold even for burglars and thieves? Probably. Minneapolis's major crime rates are lowest during winter months.[22]
Statistics are serious business, but sometimes you can have fun with them.

Putting Statistics to Good Use

Are gun-caused deaths out of control in this nation of ours, as many Americans believe? In late 1999, the federal Centers for Disease Control and Prevention reported that the latest national figures available show the rate of gun-related deaths at the lowest level in 30 years.[23]

Then is the problem youth violence? A separate Centers for Disease Control and Prevention study found violent juvenile crime at its lowest nationwide level in a decade.[24]

Well, it must be that other major crimes are up. No. An FBI report found nationwide rates of major crimes (including burglaries and such) continuing a seven-year decline that began in the early 1990s.[25]

But don't jump to the conclusion that the crime problem is over. The Milton S. Eisenhower Foundation issued a 1999 report that wakes us up to reality. The report noted that violent crime in our nation's large cities has risen by 40 percent over where it was 30 years ago.[26]
You still have to know where it's safe to walk.

The recent national declines in crime rates are encouraging—but we can do better. Numbers can help us by showing us what we are doing right, and what we are doing wrong.

Experts attribute the recent drop in major crimes to anticrime measures, a growing economy, the aging of the large baby boom population, and the decline of crack cocaine use. Experts attribute the drop in gun deaths to tougher gun-control laws and more gun-safety courses, among other things, but the Centers for Disease Control and Prevention said more studies are needed.

Good statistics can show us what does, and doesn't, work in many areas. And these statistics can make good news stories along the way. Note that we said *good* statistics, which leads to . . .

The GIGO Reminder

Robert Samuelson, *Newsweek*'s economics columnist, advises us:

"If you are going to use a number, you'd better know where it comes from, how reliable it is and whether it means what it seems to mean. The garbage-in, garbage-out problem has been with us a long time. Or as British economist Sir Josiah Stamp (1880–1941) once put it: 'The government [is] very keen on amassing statistics. They collect them, add them, raise them to the nth power, take the cube root and prepare wonderful diagrams. But you must never forget that every one of these figures comes in the first instance from the village watchman, who just puts down what he damn well pleases.'"[27]

Data-gathering is *far* better today, but there are still some garbagemen.

This Book's Bottom Line

Author Darrell Huff says: "A difference is a difference only if it makes a difference."[28] We hope this manual will make a difference in how you think about numbers in the news and about all the statistics that affect our lives.

The emphasis has necessarily been on the ways that statistics can go wrong, the ways that scientific studies can go wrong, the ways that reporting can go wrong. If you've read the entire book, you might decide to believe nothing you hear. That would be what statisticians call a Type II error: Failing to detect a result when one is there, or, in practical terms, disbelieving the truth. Believing everything would be a Type I error: Believing untruth.

All testing, including a reporter's testing of truth, involves tradeoffs. If you're too gullible, you make too many Type I errors. If you're too skeptical or even cynical—the sad person who believes nothing—you may make too many Type II errors.

Reporters and the public alike can avoid those extremes. We reporters can report studies, polls, and other statistical claims in ways that will allow our readers and viewers to more fully appreciate their worth, as well as their limitations. And the public can learn to read and listen more wisely.

Checklist—See "What Makes a Good Reporter?" in the Appendix.

Appendix: Quick-Reference Guides

Working the Web

Reporters often need national and other statistics to make comparisons and to give a full picture about some developments. The Internet is a tremendous resource for reporters seeking statistics and other information. Of course, any information is only as good as its source. While a list of potentially useful web sites is too long for this book, here are some starting points that we recommend:

Centers for Disease Control and Prevention—*www.cdc.gov.* This federal agency's web site offers statistics and other information about numerous diseases.

Food and Drug Administration—*www.fda.gov.* This site has information about drugs, food labels, health frauds, medical devices, and more.

Clinical Trials—*www.clinicaltrials.gov.* This National Institutes of Health site has much information about drug trials and other patient studies.

U.S. government's "Big Window"—*www.fedstats.gov.* This site links to numerous federal statistical sites dealing with health, the census, education, and much more.

American Heart Association—*www.americanheart.org.* Heart disease is the nation's number one killer. This web site puts related statistics and other information only a click away.

American Cancer Society—*www.cancer.org.* This site does for the nation's second leading killer what the heart association's site does for heart disease.

Medical ethics—*www.med.upenn.edu/bioethics.* Medical studies can raise cost-effectiveness, informed consent, and other ethical issues. The renowned bioethics team at the University of Pennsylvania sponsors this web site. It links users to bioethics resources across the nation.

Reporting a Disease Outbreak

Outbreaks of food-borne illnesses, meningitis, and many other infectious diseases require reporters to ask specialized, numbers-probing questions. Dr. Michael Osterholm, former state epidemiologist for Minnesota, helped prepare this checklist of questions to consider:

To assess the size of the outbreak—How many people are ill? How many are confirmed cases, how many are probable cases, how many are only possible cases? How many more cases are expected? Could more cases already have occurred, just not yet been reported?

To assess the severity of the illness—How many people (if any) have been hospitalized or have died? What are the symptoms? How ill do people get? Have long is a person likely to remain ill? If applicable: What's the fatality rate in a typical outbreak?

To determine who is at risk and how the illness is treated—Is the cause (if known) a virus, bacterium, or other infectious agent? What's known about it? Is an unusual strain involved? How is it treated? Which groups are most vulnerable (young or old, people with other medical problems, etc.)?

To assess how (and how easily) the disease is spread and what to do about it—Is it spread through personal contact, by mosquitoes, through food, or in some other way?

Is this the time of year that this disease normally spreads? How easily is it spread? How long does a patient remain infectious—capable of spreading the virus to others?

Is a vaccine available? Who should get it? Can good hand-washing help? Other protective steps? (Hand-washing is particularly important for food-borne illnesses.)

Are there both primary and secondary cases? (*Example:* The primary cases can be people who ate a specific company's contaminated food product; secondary cases can occur when these people spread the "bug" to others in their families.) When appropriate: How many cases are primary? Secondary? What should people do to prevent primary cases? Secondary cases?

To help people assess whether their risk has passed— What is the incubation period—the time that it takes for a person to become ill after exposure to a particular virus or other infectious agent? This may reassure some people that their risk of becoming ill is past. And knowing the incubation period may help determine when the risk of any new cases occurring is over.

To put the outbreak in perspective—How many cases occur in a typical year in the state? Nation? How many this year?

To understand the investigation and what it may learn—When did the first case occur? When did the first case get reported to health authorities? Have you questioned people in a healthy comparison group? (This is to see how the people who became ill differ in what they've eaten, where they've traveled, or in some other way.) What do lab tests show? Other investigative techniques? Where do you think the virus (or other infectious agent) came from? Have there been similar outbreaks recently in other states? Is there a link?

To make sure you have touched all bases—Ask at the end of an interview or press conference, What else should the public know?

Checklists for Studies and Polls

Eight Key Areas for Assessing a Study

1. Was the study *large enough* to pass statistical muster? Are the findings unlikely to be due to chance alone?

2. Was the study *designed well?* Could unintentional bias have affected the results?

3. Did the study *last long enough?*

4. Are there *other possible explanations* for the findings? Any other reasons to question the conclusions?

5. Do the conclusions *fit with other scientific evidence?* If not, why?

6. Do I have the *full picture?*

7. Have the findings been *checked by other experts?*

8. *What now?* What's the potential from the research? What problems might pop up?

See Chapter 5, "Questions You Can Ask." Other details are throughout this book.

Four Key Areas for Assessing a Poll

1. The people who are interviewed must be a *random sample* of the population that the poll's findings will apply to.

2. The *margin of sampling error* must be respected.

3. The *questions* asked must be fair—not tilted toward a specific answer.

4. Remember: The results are only a *snapshot in time.*

See Chapter 10, "Polls: Measuring What We Think."

What Makes a Good Reporter?

The Council for the Advancement of Science Writing asked Victor Cohn (coauthor of this book), shortly before his death, to jot down his thoughts on what makes a good medical reporter. His advice, in general terms, can serve as checklist for what makes a good reporter in any field:

A good medical reporter is, first of all, a reporter after a story, not just a medical story but an interesting and important story.

A good medical reporter also has fun, fun talking to some of the world's most dedicated and interesting people, fun writing copy that zings and captures the reader, fun that injects passion into into the job, for it is a job that needs passion.

A good medical reporter reports for people, not for doctors, not for scientists, not even for editors or news directors.

A good medical reporter is privileged to contribute to the great fabric of news that democracy requires. There is no more important job than giving people the information they need to work, to survive, to enjoy life, to participate in and maintain a free and democratic society.

The Council for the Advancement of Science Writing has established the annual Victor Cohn Prize for Excellence in Medical Science Reporting. See *www.casw.org.*

Notes

BOOK CITATIONS

The full citations for some frequently cited books may be found in the bibliography.

INTERVIEWS

Unless otherwise indicated, quotations from the following are from interviews: Drs. Michael Osterholm, Infection Control Advisory Network, Inc. (ican, inc.); John C. Bailar III, Peter Braun, Harvey Fineberg, Thomas A. Louis, Frederick Mosteller, and Marvin Zelen, at Harvard School of Public Health when interviewed; H. Jack Geiger, City University of New York; and Arnold Relman, *New England Journal of Medicine*.

QUOTATIONS FROM SEMINARS

Two other important sources for this manual were Drs. Peter Montague at Princeton University (director, Hazardous Waste Research Program) and Michael Greenberg at Rutgers University (director, Public Policy and Education Hazardous and Toxic Substances Research Center). Quotations are from their talks at symposiums titled "Public Health and the Environment: The Journalist's Dilemma," sponsored by the Council for the Advancement of Science Writing (CASW) at Syracuse University, April 1982; St. Louis, March 1983; and Ohio State University, April 1984.

CHAPTER 1 / WHERE WE CAN DO BETTER

1. Dorothy Nelkin, background paper in *Science in the Streets: Report of the Twentieth Century Fund Task Force on the Communications of Scientific Risk* (New York: Priority Press, 1984).
2. From many sources on Love Canal, including Marvin S. Legator, "You Can Do It Too," in *Health Detective's Handbook,* ed. Legator, Harper, and Scott.
3. Meyer, *Precision Journalism.*
4. "SRP [Savannah River Plant] link to diseases not valid," *Atlanta Journal-Constitution,* 14 August 1983.
5. Vogt, *Making Health Decisions.*
6. From many sources, including National Cancer Institute, *Cancer Prevention Awareness Survey,* Technical Report, NIH Publication 84-2677, February 1984.
7. *Cancer Facts & Figures 2000,* American Cancer Society, Page 32.
8. Jay A. Winsten, "Science and the Media: The Boundaries of Truth," *Health Affairs* (Spring 1985): 5–23.

CHAPTER 2 / THE CERTAINTY OF UNCERTAINTY

* Trans fatty acids, sometimes called just trans fats, are liquid fats that have been turned into solids. They are often found in margarine and baked goods.
1. Sheryl Gay Stolberg, "FDA Wants More Fat Facts on Food Labels," *New York Times,* 13 November 1999. The Food and Drug Administration offers food-labeling information at *www.fda.gov.*
2. From many news reports, including "Absolutely No Doubt," *Time,* 1 July 1985.
3. "Guidelines for the Cancer-Related Checkup: Recommendations and Rationale," *Ca* (an American Cancer Society journal), July–August 1980. And *Cancer Facts and Figures 2000,* American Cancer Society, Page 17.
4. Two reports and an editorial in the *Journal of the American Medical Association* 283, no. 1 (5 January 2000): 81–93, 108–9. Also news reports, including Denise Grady, "New Test for Cancer Surpasses the Pap One, Studies Show," *New York Times,* 5 January 2000.
5. Marvin Zelen talk at Council for the Advancement of Science Writing (CASW) seminar "New Horizons of Science," Cambridge, Mass., November 1982.
6. Vogt, *Making Health Decisions.*
7. From many sources, including John T. Bruer, "Methodological Rigor and Citation Frequency in Patient Compliance Literature," *American Journal of Public Health* 72, no. 10 (October 1982): 1119–24;

"Despite Guidelines, Many Lung Cancer Trials Poorly Conducted," *Internal Medicine News* (1 January 1984); Rebecca DerSimonian et al., "Reporting on Methods in Clinical Trials," *New England Journal of Medicine* 306, no. 22 (3 June 1982): 1332–37; Kenneth S. Warren in *Coping*, ed. Warren.
    8. Friedman, *Primer.*
    9. Frederick Mosteller in *Coping*, ed. Warren.

CHAPTER 3 / TESTING THE EVIDENCE

*There is another unrelated use of the word "power." Scientists commonly speak of increasing or raising some quantity *by a power of* 2, or 3, or 100, or whatever. "Power" here means the product you get when you multiply a number by itself one or more times. Thus, in $2 \times 2 = 4$, two has been raised to the second power. In $2 \times 2 \times 2 = 8$, two has been raised to the third power. When you think about 200 to the 100th power, you see the need for the shorthand.
    **To a statistician, a population doesn't necessarily mean a group of people. Statistically, a population is any group or collection of pertinent units—units with one or more pertinent characteristics in common. They may be people, events, objects, records, test scores, or physiological values (such as blood pressure readings). Statisticians also use the term universe for a whole group of people or units under study.
    1. John Allen Paulos, mathematics professor at Temple University, in an op-ed page article, *New York Times*, 2 November 1999.
    2. Robert Young, Fox Chase Cancer Center, Philadelphia, personal communication.
    3. Robert Hooke, *How to Tell the Liars From the Statisticians* (New York: Marcel Dekker, 1983).
    4. Mosteller talk at the Council for the Advancement of Science Writing seminar "New Horizons of Science."
    5. Zelen, "Innovations in the Design of Clinical Trials in Breast Cancer," in *Breast Cancer Research and Treatment*, no. 3 (1983), Proceedings of Fifth Annual San Antonio Breast Cancer Symposium.
    6. Friedman, *Primer.*
    7. David S. Salsburg, "The Religion of Statistics as Practiced in Medical Journals," *American Statistician* 39, no. 3 (August 1985): 220–22.
    8. John Bailar, "Science, Statistics and Deception," *Annals of Internal Medicine* 104, no. 2 (February 1986): 259–60.
    9. Vogt, *Making Health Decisions.*
    10. Meyer, *Precision Journalism.*
    11. J. A. Freiman, cited by Mosteller in *Coping*, ed. Warren.

12. Alvin R. Feinstein, "Epidemiology: Challenges and Controversies," in *1983 Encyclopedia Britannica Medical and Health Annual* (Chicago: Encyclopedia Britannica, 1983).

13. David L. Sackett in *Clinical Trials,* ed. Shapiro and Louis.

14. David Hemenway, quoted in a Harvard School of Public Health staff newsletter, November 1983.

15. Thomas Chalmers in *Clinical Trials,* ed. Shapiro and Louis.

16. Henry K. Beecher, *Measurement of Subjective Responses: Quantitative Effects of Drugs* (New York: Oxford University Press, 1959).

17. Vogt, *Making Health Decisions.*

18. Hooke, *How to Tell the Liars.*

19. Ibid.

20. Friedman, *Primer.*

21. Department of Health, Education and Welfare, *The Health Consequences of Smoking: A Report of the Surgeon General,* 1980.

22. James Trifel, "Odds are Against Your Beating the Law of Averages," *Smithsonian,* September 1984, 66–75.

23. Friedman, *Primer.*

24. Stephen Jay Gould, "The Median Isn't the Message," *Discover,* June 1985, 40–42.

CHAPTER 4 / WHAT'S A GOOD STUDY?

*Even if the clinical trials don't work out, that doesn't mean that the preceding laboratory and animal studies were in vain. They provide a growing store of knowledge that may lead to future research, with the potential for new treatment approaches or for new prevention strategies. In addition, research that may not appear to have any human applications may turn out otherwise. Studies of retrovirus in animals were extremely helpful when it discovered that HIV, the virus that causes AIDS, is a retrovirus. As we noted in Chapter 2, science is always building on itself. And this can happen in unpredictable ways.

1. Jay A. Winsten, "Science and the Media; the Boundaries of Truth," *Health Affairs* (Spring 1985): 5–23.

2. Much of the discussion about disease outbreaks is based on an interview with Dr. Michael Osterholm, former Minnesota state epidemiologist and now chairman and chief executive officer of Infection Control Advisory Network, Inc. (ican, inc.), Eden Prairie, Minn. He also is adjunct professor, University of Minnesota School of Public Health.

3. Umberto Veronesi, "Cancer Research—Developing Better Clinical Trials," *Therapaeia* (May 1984): 31.

4. Hooke, *How to Tell the Liars.*

5. Bailar, "Science, Statistics."

6. E. Cuyler Hammond, "Smoking in Relation to Death Rates of One Million Men and Women" in *Epidemiological Approaches to the Study of Cancer and Other Chronic Diseases,* ed. W. Haenszel, Department of Health, Education and Welfare, National Cancer Institute Monograph no. 19, January 1986.

7. Eugene D. Robin, *Medical Care Can Be Hazardous to Your Health* (New York: Harper and Row, 1986).

8. Paul Meier, "The Biggest Public Health Experiment Ever," in *Statistics,* ed. Tanur et al.

9. The AIDS statistics are from *Health, United States, 1999.* Annual editions of this excellent source book contain extensive statistics on many aspects of health. The book is prepared by the federal National Center for Health Statistics and sold by the U.S. Superintendent of Documents.

10. A good source for information on Reye Syndrome (and many diseases) is *www.cdc.gov,* the web site of the Centers for Disease Control and Prevention.

CHAPTER 5 / QUESTIONS YOU CAN ASK

*Frederick Mosteller disagrees with our occasional reference to good sense or common sense. If something is a common sense idea, he says, "surely all would have thought of it. So it must be uncommon sense after all." He makes good sense.

1. Christine Gorman, "Still High on Fiber," *Time,* 1 February 1999.

2. *Morbidity and Mortality Weekly Report* (Centers for Disease Control and Prevention, Atlanta) 30 (June 1981): 250–52.

3. Vogt, *Making Health Decisions.*

4. Barbara McNeil, et al., "On the Elicitation of Preferences for Alternative Therapies," *New England Journal of Medicine* 306, no. 21 (27 May 1982): 1259–62.

5. David Sackett in *Coping,* ed. Warren.

6. Mosteller talk at CASW seminar.

7. Bailar, "Science, Statistics."

8. Various news reports, including *Wall Street Journal,* 11 October 1999.

9. Arnold Relman in *Clinical Trials,* ed. Shapiro and Louis.

10. Robert Boruch, quoted in "Taking the Measure, or Mismeasure, of It All," *New York Times,* 28 August 1984.

11. Sackett in *Clinical Trials,* ed. Shapiro and Louis.

CHAPTER 6 / TESTS AND TESTING

1. Gina Kolata, "Large Study Urged for New Method of Detecting Lung Cancer," *New York Times*, 27 October 1999.
2. Gardiner Harris, in-depth report, "After Vaccine's Recall, Regulators Look for Holes in the Safety Net," *Wall Street Journal*, 18 October 1999.
3. Barbara G. Valanis and Carol S. Perlman, "Home Pregnancy Tests: Prevalence of Use, False-Negative Rates and Compliance With Instructions," *American Journal of Public Health* 72, no. 9 (September 1982): 1034–36.
4. Friedman, *Primer*.
5. John Urquhart and Klaus Heilman, *Risk Watch: The Odds of Life* (New York: Facts on File, 1984).
6. Friedman, *Primer*.
7. Interdisciplinary Panel on Carcinogenicity, "Criteria for Evidence of Chemical Carcinogenicity," *Science* 225 (17 August 1984): 682–87.

CHAPTER 7 / VITAL STATISTICS

1. Bernard Guyer et al., "Annual Summary of Vital Statistics," *Pediatrics* 104, no. 6 (December 1999): 1229–45.
2. Robert D. Hershey Jr., "Rise in Death Rate After New Year Is Tied to Will to See 2000," front-page article in *New York Times*, 15 January 2000.
3. In part from Vogt, *Making Health Decisions*.
4. Friedman, *Primer*.
5. Hammond, "Smoking."
6. The primary source of cancer statistics in this chapter is the SEER program of the National Cancer Institute. The American Cancer Society also uses SEER data. For SEER reports, see (a) *www-seer.ims.nci.nih.gov*; (b) Phyllis Wingo et al., "Annual Report to the Nation on the Status of Cancer," by experts at NCI, the American Cancer Society, and the Centers for Disease Control and Prevention, *Journal of the National Cancer Institute* 91 no. 8 (21 April 1999), 675–90; (c) The American Cancer Society's *Cancer Facts and Figures 2000*.
7. NCI press release, 20 April 1999, and Wingo et al., "Annual Report to the Nation on the Status of Cancer," cited above.
8. NCI press release, 20 April 1999, and *Cancer Facts and Figures for African Americans*, American Cancer Society.
9. Kelly-Anne Phillips et al., "Putting the Risk of Breast Cancer in Perspective," *New England Journal of Medicine* 340, no. 2 (14 January 1999): 141–44.

10. Barbara B. Harrell, "The One-in-Nine Risk of Breast Cancer," letter to editor, *New England Journal of Medicine* 340, no. 23 (10 June 1999): 1839–40.

CHAPTER 8 / HEALTH PLANS AND HOSPITALS

The information on hospital death rates is based in part on an April 1987 health executive training program sponsored by the American Medical Review Research Center and on a paper and sample questions a coauthor of this book (Cohn) prepared. Among speakers whose knowledge we drew on were Andrew Webber, American Medical Peer Review Organization; and Drs. Robert Brook, University of California at Los Angeles and Rand Corporation; John Bunker, Stanford Medical Center; Mark Chassin, Rand Corporation; Carlos Enriquez, Peer Review Organization of New Jersey; Sanford Feldman and William Moncrief, Jr., California Medical Review, Inc.; Harold Luft, University of California at San Francisco; Marilyn Moon, American Association of Retired Persons; Helen Smits, University of Connecticut; and Sidney Wolfe, Public Citizen Health Research Group.

1. The health-plans section is based on extensive interviews by Victor Cohn. A detailed look at the subject is available in booklet form: *A Newsperson's Guide to Reporting Health Plan Performance*, prepared by Cohn and distributed by the American Association of Health Plans, Washington, D.C., 2000.

2. From many news reports, 30 November 1999.

3. Cohn, *A Newsperson's Guide to Reporting Health Plan Performance*, page 13.

4. R. Adams Dudley, "Selective Referral to High-Volume Hospitals," and an accompanying editorial, *Journal of the American Medical Association* 283, No. 9 (1 March 2000): 1159–1166 and 1191–93.

CHAPTER 9 / OUR ENVIRONMENT AND MEASURING ALL RISKS

*There was a partial core meltdown at the Three Mile Island nuclear power plant in Pennsylvania in 1979. The Bhopal, India, chemical plant explosion in 1984 took more than 3,800 lives. The Exxon Valdez's massive oil spill off Alaska was in 1989.

**In this chapter we drew substantially on the presentations, and often the words, of Dr. Michael Greenberg at Rutgers University and Dr. Peter Montague at Princeton University at science writers' symposiums. Cass Peterson of the *Washington Post* and others added to the questions that reporters can ask.

1. Baruch Fischhoff, "Reporting on Environmental and Health Risks," in *NewsBackgrounder,* Foundation for American Communications.

2. David Harris, "Health Department: Enemy or Champion of the People?" (editorial), *American Journal of Public Health* 74, no. 5 (May 1984): 428–30.

3. Peter Montague quoted in Cohn, *Reporting on Risk,* page 38.

4. Vogt, *Making Health Decisions.*

5. Dr. Genevieve Matanoski, Johns Hopkins University, in a talk at the conference titled "Toxics and the News," sponsored by the Foundation for American Communications and the Gannett Foundation, Princeton, N.J., May 1984.

6. "Can Science Deal With Environmental Uncertainties," *Conservation Foundation Letter,* January 1982.

7. Barbara S. Hulka, "When Is the Evidence for 'No Association' Sufficient?" (editorial), *Journal of the American Medical Association* 252, no. 1 (6 July 1984): 811–12.

8. Kenneth Rothman, Boston University, quoted in Gina Kolata, "Cell Phone Studies See No Link to Brain Cancer," *New York Times,* 20 December 2000. Other information is from this and other news reports.

9. Timothy Jones et al., "Mass Psychogenic Illness Attributed to Toxic Exposure at a High School," *New England Journal of Medicine* 342, no. 2 (13 January 2000): 96–100.

10. Nelkin, background paper; and *Science in the Streets.*

11. Gary D. Friedman, personal communication.

12. Jim Detjen, talk at CASW seminars "Public Health and the Environment."

13. Douglas R. Hofstadter, *Mathematical Themas* (New York: Basic Books, 1985).

14. "Consumer's Guide to Radon Reduction" and "A Citizen's Guide to Radon." The brochures are by the U.S. Environmental Protection Agency (EPA).

15. Cohn, *Reporting on Risk,* page 55.

16. EPA news release, 20 March 2000. Much information on environmental topics is available from the EPA web site, *www.epa.gov.*

17. John Ullmann, quoted in Cohn, *Reporting on Risk,* page 20.

18. Nelkin, background paper.

19. Detjen, quoted in Cohn, *Reporting on Risk,* page 54.

CHAPTER 10 / POLLS

1. Daniel Goleman, in-depth report on polling techniques, "Pollsters Enlist Psychologists in Quest for Unbiased Results," *New York Times,* 7 September 1993.

2. "How Poll Was Conducted," *Star Tribune* of Minneapolis–St. Paul, 28 November 1999.

3. "How the Poll Was Conducted," *New York Times*, 9 January 1987.

4. "How Poll Was Conducted," *Star Tribune*, cited above.

5. Associated Press report on the Pew Research Center poll, 22 July 1999.

6. Goleman, cited above.

7. These examples, and some general observations for this chapter, are based on an interview with Rob Daves, director of the Minnesota Poll at the *Star Tribune* of Minneapolis–St. Paul.

8. Burns Roper, quoted in "Private Opinions on Public Opinion: Question Is, What Is the Question?," *New York Times*, 24 August 1994.

9. Dane Smith, "The Stretch Run: It's Up for Grabs," *Star Tribune* of Minneapolis–St. Paul, 1 November 1998.

10. Louis Harris, quoted on National Public Radio, 8 November 1984.

11. Richard Wirthlin, quoted in "Public Opinion Polls: Are They Science or Art?" *Los Angeles Times-Washington Post* News Service, 27 August 1984.

12. This section is based on various news reports on election day, 7 November 2000, and in its aftermath. The primary sources were the Associated Press (for the Frankovic and Ortiz quotations on 8 November), the *New York Times*, *USA Today*, and the *Wall Street Journal*. Howard Kurtz wrote an excellent recap in the *Washington Post* on 22 December 2000.

13. The Minnesota Poll's Daves offers more detailed information on percentage points, and other help on writing and editing poll articles, in *Contemporary Editing*, by Cecilia Friend, Don Challenger, and Katherine C. McAdams, NTC Publishing Group, pages 354–55.

14. Robert Samuelson, "The Joy of Statistics," *Newsweek*, 4 November 1985.

15. Lewis Cope, "Save Your Life," five-part series in *Star Tribune* of Minneapolis–St. Paul; each Thursday, 8 October through 5 November 1992.

16. Shere Hite, *Women and Love: A Cultural Revolution in Progress* (New York: Alfred A. Knopf, 1987); Sally Squires, "Modem Couples Say They're Happy Together," *Washington Post*, 27 October 1987; David Streitfeld, "Shere Hite and the Trouble With Numbers," *Washington Post*, 10 November 1987; "Hite Lacks Depth, Says Rival Poll," *New York Daily News*, 29 October 1987; Arlie Russell Hochschild, "Why Can't a Man Be More Like a Woman?" *New York Times Book Review*, 15 November 1987; "Men Aren't Her Only Problem," *Newsweek*, 23 November 1987.

17. Ralph Kinney Bennett, *Reader's Digest*, interview with author.

CHAPTER 11 / POLITICS, YOUR POCKETBOOK, AND PLENTY MORE

1. Nancy Lyon Spruill, "Perspective: Politics by the Numbers," *Washington Post*, 20 September 1984.
2. "Meat Export Rise Could Buoy Prices," *Washington Post*, 31 March 1973.
3. Daniel Seligman, "We're Drowning in Phony Statistics," *Fortune*, November 1961.
4. Anemona Hartocollis, "New Math: No One Is Below Average," *New York Times*, 20 June 1999; and "Liar, Liar, Pants on Fire," *New York Times*, 12 December 1999.
5. Malcolm Gladwell, "Murder Capital We're Not," *Washington Post*, 16 April 1989.
6. This critique is based on observations by Victor Cohn after he had been asked by a statistician, "Is the public learning anything about statistics from the O.J. Simpson trial?"
7. This section is based on various news reports about the Thomas Jefferson history case, as well as the scientific report by Eugene Foster et al. in *Nature* 396 (5 November 1998): 13–14 and 27–28. Foster further discussed the case in a letter to the editor, *New York Times*, 9 November 1998. The press's performance got a drubbing in "Vital Stats: The Numbers Behind the News," the newsletter of the Statistical Assessment Service, November 1998, which noted the headline that we cited.
8. Dennis Cauchon, "Foundation Agrees: Jefferson Probably Fathered Slave's Kids," *USA Today*, front-page in-depth article, 27 January 2000.
9. Julian L. Simon, "Probability—'Batter's Slump' and Other Illusions," *Washington Post*, 9 August 1987.
10. Mosteller, personal communication.
11. Hooke, *How to Tell the Liars*.
12. Huff, *How to Lie*.
13. "Largest Stock Funds" (table), *USA Today*, 4 January 2001.
14. Jan J. Barendregt et al., "The Health Care Cost of Smoking," *New England Journal of Medicine* 337, no. 15 (9 October 1997): 1052-57. Also, a news report on the journal article by John Schwartz, "Health Savings for Nonsmokers Disputed," *Washington Post*, 9 October 1997.
15. Spencer Rich, "A Costly Ounce of Prevention," *Washington Post*, 29 August 1993. Also, Laurie Jones, "Does Prevention Save Money?" *American Medical News*, 9 January 1995.
16. From many news reports, 19 January 2000.
17. David Cay Johnston, "Corporate Taxes Fall, but Citizens Are Paying More," *New York Times*, 20 February 2000.
18. Barry Glassner, quoted in "Reading the News Can Be Dangerous," *New York Times*, 4 November 1999.

19. I. Richard Savage, presidential address, American Statistical Association, Philadelphia, 14 August 1984.

20. "How Lobbyists Play the Numbers Game," *Newsweek*, 12 February 1990.

21. "Deaths in Building-Site Accidents Found to Be Highest in New York," *New York Times*, 21 September 1987.

22. Lewis Cope, "How the Weather Affects Minnesotans' Lives," *Star Tribune* of Minneapolis–St. Paul, 5 November 1985.

23. Associated Press report, 18 November, 1999; *Morbidity and Mortality Weekly Report* 48, no. 45 (19 November 1999): 1029–1034; *Health, United States, 1999* (Table 48).

24. News reports on juvenile crime, 23 November 1999.

25. Associated Press report, "Serious Crime Down 10% in First Half of Year, FBI Reports" in the *New York Times*, 22 November 1999.

26. David Vise and Lorraine Adams, "Despite Rhetoric, Violent Crime Climbs," *Washington Post*, 5 December 1999.

27. Robert Samuelson, "The Joy of Statistics," *Newsweek*, 4 November 1985.

28. Huff, *How to Lie*.

Glossary

Absolute survival (or **observed survival**): The actual proportion of a group still living after a certain time. Often compared with relative survival. *See also* **Relative survival.**

Actuarial method. *See* **Life table method.**

Adjusted rate (or **standardized rate**): A way of comparing two groups that differ in some important variable (e.g., age) by mathematically eliminating the effect of that variable. *See also* **Crude rate.**

Analytic study: An observational study that seeks to analyze or explain the occurrence of a disease or characteristic in a population.

Attack rate: The incidence of new cases of a disease in a population, often during an epidemic.

Background (or **background rate**): The already occurring rate of some physiological effect or physical phenomenon (such as radiation) in a population or locality. This is distinguished from the rate added by some additional influence.

Bias: The influence of irrelevant or even spurious factors or association on a result or conclusion.

Blinding: A method of keeping study participants and, if possible, researchers unaware of which participants are in an experimental group (those getting a new drug, e.g.) and which are in a control group (those getting an older drug or a placebo). The aim is to prevent people's hopes and expectations from affecting the reported results.

Case-control study: A study that compares individuals affected by a disease with a comparable group of people who do not have that disease, to seek possible causes or associations.

Chi-square test: One commonly used mathematical technique to measure the probability that what is observed didn't occur by chance alone.

Clinical trial: A research study to determine whether an experimental treatment works, or to see whether there are new ways to use a known treatment. Clinical trials answer questions about the safety and effectiveness of drugs, other treatments, diagnostic procedures, and vaccines. At its best, a clinical trial is a study involving two (or more) comparable,

195

randomly selected groups; for example, an experimental group that gets an experimental drug, and an untreated (or differently treated) control group. *See also* **Control group, Crossover study, External controls,** and **Historical controls.**

Cohort study (or **incidence study**): A study of a group of people, or cohort, followed over time to see how some disease or diseases develop.

Confidence interval (or **confidence limits**): In an estimate or measurement of a result in a sample, the range within which the truth probably lies.

Confounder(s) (or **confounding variables** or **covariables**): Other factors or explanations that may affect a result or conclusion.

Control group: A comparison group. A group of individuals used by a researcher as a standard for comparison, to see how they differ from an experimental group (such as people receiving a new treatment). *See also* **Blinding.**

Correlation: The extent to which two or more variables in an association are related. For example, the extent by which one variable changes in response to changes in another. *See also* **Linear relationship.**

Crossover study: A clinical trial in which the same patients get two or more treatments in succession, thus acting as their own controls.

Crude rate: The actual rate of cases of a disease in a population, without adjustment. *See also* **Adjusted rate.**

Denominator: The number or population representing the total uni-

verse in which an event might happen.

Descriptive study: A study that describes the incidence, prevalence, and mortality of a disease in a population.

Design: The plan or method of a study or experiment.

Distribution: The summary of a collection of measurements or values showing how the results of a study, for example, fall along a scale.

Dose-response relationship: The relationship between the dose of some drug or other agent, or the extent of some exposure, and a physiological response. A dose-response effect means that the effect increases with the dose.

Ecological fallacy: An assumption, based on observing a number of cases in a population, that there is a cause-and-effect relationship that also applies to populations in other locations.

Ecological study: In epidemiology, a study seeking a relationship between illness and environmental conditions.

Epidemiology: The study of cases and patterns to seek the causes of health and diseases.

Excess risk (or **excess rate**): An increased rate due to some known or unknown cause.

Expected rate: A rate adjusted to eliminate the effect of age or some other variable. This can be used for comparison with a rate in a similar population subjected to same effect. For example, the lung cancer rate in nonsmokers can be compared to the rate in smokers, adjusted to eliminate age differences in the two groups.

Experimental group: The treated group in a study, in contrast to an untreated or more conventionally treated control group.

External controls: Use of results of other studies (rather than a simultaneously observed control group) to gauge the effects of some treatment.

False negative: The failure to find a result or effect when there is one. *Treatment study:* The false indication that a medical treatment is not working when it really is working. *Diagnostic test:* The false indication that a person doesn't have the medical problem when she or he actually does have that problem. A false negative also can be called a Type II error.

False positive: Finding a result or effect when it really doesn't exist. *Treatment study:* The false indication that a medical treatment is working when it really is not working. *Diagnostic test:* The false indication that a person has a medical problem when he or she actually doesn't have that problem. A false positive also can be called a Type I error.

Gaussian curve. *See* **Normal distribution.**

Historical controls: Comparison of the results in an experimental group with results in former, often old, reports or records.

Hypothesis: A tentative statement or supposition, which may then be tested through research. *See also* **Null hypothesis.**

Incidence rate: The occurrence of some event, such as the number of individuals who get a disease, divided by a total given population per unit of time.

Independent variable: In a two-variable relationship, the underlying variable that affects the incidence of the dependent variable. Weather, for example, as it affects the incidence of colds.

Individualistic fallacy: An assumption that the results in a small and unrepresentative number of cases also apply to a larger population.

Interquartile range: The interval between the 75th and 25th percentiles in a data set. This is the middle 50 percent of a distribution, avoiding the extreme values at either end.

Intervention study: An epidemiological study in which there is some intervention in some subjects to modify a supposed cause of disease.

Inverse relationship: A negative correlation between two variables. The way that one increases as the other decreases. *Example:* a runner's average speed goes down as his or her weight goes up.

Life table method (or **actuarial method**): In a five-year study of cancer, for example, a way of predicting the final result though some of the subjects began treatment less than five years earlier. The conclusion is based on experience to date with some participants in the study and reasonable expectation for the others.

Linear relationship: A positive (or negative) correlation between two variables, showing up as a straight, steadily rising (or falling) set of data points on a graph.

Mean: The arithmetic average. The sum of all the values divided by the number of values.

Median: The value or number that divides a population into equal halves.

Meta-analysis: A way of combining the results of several studies to draw conclusions.

Mode: The most frequently occurring value in a distribution.

Morbidity rate: The incidence of a particular disease or, often, all illnesses per unit of time (often per year) in a population.

Mortality rate: The incidence of deaths per unit of time, most often per year, in a population.

Multivariate analysis: A way of studying many variables to try to understand the relationships between them. For example, a way of relating many variables in a study to find those that are truly important.

Natural experiment: An experiment of nature or a change in human habits that can be studied to draw valuable conclusions.

Nonparametric method: A technique of examining data that does not rely on a numerical distribution. For example, using a plus or minus sign rather than a count to record a result.

Normal distribution: A collection of individual values that show up in a graph as a bell-shaped (or Gaussian) curve, high in the middle and low at each end. To the layman, and in common use, anything approximating this form. To a mathematician, a curve complying with a more precise formula.

Null hypothesis: A way an investigator can scrupulously test an initial, hopeful hypothesis. The researcher hypothesizes that a

treatment, for example, has no effect, then sees if the results disprove this negative assumption.

Observational study: A study that simply observes and describes, offering clues but not a positive determination of cause and effect. *Example:* the simultaneous occurrence of acid rain and the losses in plant and animal life.

Observed rate: The actual rate of a disease or condition, without adjustment to eliminate the effect of age or other variables.

Parallel study: A clinical study comparing two similar groups simultaneously given different treatments or treatment versus no treatment.

Parameter: As most commonly used, a measurable characteristic or property.

Peer review: Evaluation of a medical or scientific report or proposal by other qualified people.

Placebo: A supposedly ineffective pill or agent used in a control group to gauge the effect of an actual treatment in another group. Experimenters often must allow for a placebo effect, a response caused by suggestion.

Population: In statistics, any group or collection of relevant units—people, events, objects, test scores, physiologic values, or whatever—from which a sample may be drawn for study.

Power: In statistics, the probability of finding an effect if one is in fact present, dependent on adequate size of the sample or population studied.

Prevalence rate: The total case rate of a disease or condition in a given population at a given time. In epidemiology, a prevalence (or current or cross-sectional) study examines the relationship between a disease and other variables in a population at a particular time.

Probability: A calculation of what may be expected, based on what has happened in the past under similar conditions.

Prospective study: A study of morbidity and mortality and other characteristics in a group while it is under study. By comparison, a retrospective study examines a group exposed in the past. Prospective studies watch diseases develop; retrospective studies look at people who already have a disease.

Protocol: The plan and rules for a study, set prior to its implementation. The protocol includes, among other things, who may participate in the study, the dosages of drugs to be used and tests to be conducted, and the duration of the study.

P **value** (or **probability value**): The probability that an observed result or effect could have occurred by chance if there had actually been no real effect.

Randomization: Division of a sample into two or more comparable groups by some random method that eliminates biased selection.

Random variation (or **chance**): The way a coin will successively turn up heads or tails if flipped in just the same way.

Range: A measure of spread; for example, the spread between the highest and lowest values in a distribution.

Rate: The proportion of some disease or condition in a group per unit of time, with a numerator and denominator (stated or implied) telling us "so many per so many per year or other unit of time."

Regression (or **regression analysis**): A mathematical method commonly used to determine how greatly various other or independent variables affect a dependent variable or outcome.

Regression toward the mean: The tendency for an unusually high or low value at one time to be less extreme at a second measurement.

Relative risk (or **risk ratio**): A comparison of two morbidity or mortality rates by calculating the ratio of one to the other.

Relative survival: This is a mathematically produced (in statistical parlance, adjusted) figure that is calculated to show the chance of survival from one disease alone (commonly cancer), rather than survival from the many diseases and causes that always affect a population. Relative survival thus appears longer, as a rule, than actual (known as absolute or observed) survival.

Reliability: The reproducibility of a result when a test or experiment is repeated.

Retrospective study. *See* **Prospective study.**

Risk assessment: A quantitative estimate of the degree of hazard to a population presented by some agent or technology or decision. A risk-benefit assessment attempts to weigh possible risks against possible benefits.

Sample: A part of a population, selected by a technique called sampling, to represent the whole population.

Self-controlled study: A clinical study in which the subjects (participants) act as their own controls, with the researcher comparing periods of treatment with periods of either no treatment or some other treatment.

Sensitivity/Specificity: *Sensitivity* is the ability of a test to avoid false negatives; its ability to identify a disease or condition in those who have it. *Specificity* is a test's ability to avoid mistaken identifications—that is, false positives.

Significance: In an experiment or clinical trial, statistical significance means there is only a small statistical probability that the same result could have been found by chance alone.

Specificity. *See* **Sensitivity/Specificity.**

Spread, measurement of. *See* **Range.**

Statistics: As a scientific discipline or method, a way of gathering and analyzing data to extract information, seek causation, and calculate probabilities.

Stratification: Separation of a sample or population into subgroups, according to some characteristic.

Strength: Statistically, the strength of an association. The greater the odds of an effect, the stronger the association.

Survival. *See* **Absolute survival** and **Relative survival.**

Type I error. *See* **False positive.**

Type II error. *See* **False negative.**

Universe: A population. The whole group of people or units under consideration.

Validity: The truth or accuracy of a statistic or an experimental result or conclusion.

Variability (or **variation**): Fluctuation from measurement to measurement, common in all measurement.

Variable: Any factor, measurement, characteristic, or event that can vary—and, in a study or experiment, can affect the outcome.

Vital statistics: The systematically collected statistics on births, deaths, marriages, divorces, and other life events. More broadly, the statistics of life, health, disease, and death. In particular, the statistics that measure progress, or lack of it, against disease.

Bibliography

Statistics Texts and Manuals

Freedman, David, Robert Pisani, and Roger Purves. *Statistics.* New York: W. W. Norton, 1978. A complete, readable, and even entertaining statistics text with many examples and anecdotes and a conversational style.

Leaverton, Paul F. *A Review of Biostatistics: A Program for Self-Instruction.* 2d ed. Boston: Little, Brown, 1978. A course of instruction in 87 concise pages.

Moore, David S. *Statistics: Concepts and Controversies.* 2d ed. New York: W, H. Freeman, 1986. A full-size work that lives up to its blurb: "the heart of statistics with careful explanations and real-life examples, avoiding unnecessarily complicated mathematics."

Moses, Lincoln. *Think and Explain with Statistics.* Reading, Mass.: Addison-Wesley, 1986. By a Stanford professor and one of American statistics' major figures. A popular statistics text that is strong on practical use of statistics.

White, David M., and Seymour Levine. *Elementary Statistics for Journalists.* New York: Macmillan, 1954. Professor Michael Greenberg at Rutgers calls this "the best introduction for journalists who have no background nor any time to take a course."

Youden, W. J. *Experimentation and Measurement.* Washington, D.C.: U.S. Government Printing Office, 1984. We recommend this as a supplemental source. Written by a consultant to the National Bureau of Standards, it focuses on use

of statistics in measurement but also has many valuable sections on statistics in general.

Zeisel, Hans. *Say It with Figures.* 6th ed. New York: Harper and
Row, 1985. Both a text and a guide to understanding—and
questioning—social statistics.

Epidemiology Texts—In Fact, Simple Statistics Courses

Friedman, Gary D. *Primer of Epidemiology.* 3d ed. New York:
McGraw Hill, 1987. A Kaiser epidemiologist and biostatisti-
cian, Friedman covers much of statistics, with examples
from medicine and epidemiology. A treasure, concise and
easy to read and follow.

Lilienfeld, Abraham, and David E. Lillienfeld. *Foundations of
Epidemiology.* 2d ed. New York: Oxford University Press,
1980. A standard, for good reason.

*On the Statistics of Real-Life Situations—Good-Reading Companions
to Texts*

Campbell, Stephen K. *Flaws and Fallacies in Statistical Thinking.*
Englewood Cliffs, N.J.: Prentice-Hall, 1974. The emphasis is
on recognizing statistical frauds and whoppers, intentional
or otherwise, and distinguishing between valid and faulty
reasoning.

Huff, Darrell. *How to Lie with Statistics.* New York: W. W. Norton,
1954. Short, provocative, amusing.

Tanur, Judith M., ed., and by Frederick Mosteller, William H.
Kruskal, Erich L. Lehmann, Richard F. Link, Richard S.
Pieters, and Gerald R. Rising. *Statistics: A Guide to the
Unknown.* 3d ed. Pacific Grove, Calif.: Wadsworth and
Brooks-Cole. An anomaly, a good work produced by a com-
mittee. A series of chapters on the practical applications of
almost every branch of statistics, from surveys to medical
experiments to weather to sports.

Vogt, Thomas M. *Making Health Decisions: An Epidemiologic
Perspective on Staying Well.* Chicago: Nelson-Hall, 1983. For

the general reader or the journalist, guidance and good reading on "making sound judgments about claims and counter-claims" about health and disease.

Weaver, Warren. *Lady Luck: The Theory of Probability.* Garden City, N.Y: Doubleday Anchor Books, 1963. All you want to know about probability, from the amusingly anecdotal to the technical.

On Applying Statistics and Polling Methods to Reporting

Meyer, Philip. *Precision Journalism: A Reporter's Introduction to Social Science Methods.* 2d ed. Bloomington: Indiana University Press, 1979. The first and now classic work in this area, by a longtime *Detroit Free Press* and Knight reporter and editor, who became a professor at the University of North Carolina, Chapel Hill.

On Statistics in Medicine, Biomedical Research, and Clinical Trials (Written for Researchers and Physicians but with Much Rich Detail for Conscientious Medical Reporters)

Bailar, John C., III, and Frederick Mosteller, eds. *Medical Uses of Statistics.* Waltham, Mass.: NEJM Books, 1986. This grew out of a series in the *New England Journal of Medicine.*

Inglefinger, J. A., Frederick Mosteller, L. A. Thibodeau, and J. H. Ware. *Biostatistics in Clinical Medicine.* 2d ed. New York: Macmillan, 1986.

Shapiro, Stanley H., and Thomas A. Louis, eds. *Clinical Trials: Issues and Approaches.* New York: Marcel Dekker, 1983.

Warren, Kenneth S. *Coping With the Biomedical Literature: A Primer for the Scientist and the Clinician.* New York: Praeger, 1981.

On Health Hazards

Legator, Marvin S., Barbara L. Harper, and Michael J. Scott, eds. *The Health Detective's Handbook: A Guide to the Investigation of*

Environmental Health Hazards by Nonprofessionals. Baltimore: Johns Hopkins University Press, 1985. A marvelous practical guide for concerned citizens and inquiring reporters.

Related Publications by Victor Cohn, Coauthor of This Book

Cohn, Victor. *Reporting on Risk: Getting It Right in an Age of Risk.* Washington, D.C.: The Media Institute, 1990. A book about environmental and related risk reporting, which expands on the environmental chapter in *News & Numbers.*

Cohn, Victor. *A Newsperson's Guide to Reporting Health Plan Performance.* A booklet prepared independently by Cohn and distributed by the American Association of Health Plans, Washington, D.C. Published in 2000.

Index

(n*, n**, and n plus a number represent the note on the page.)